walking
with GOD

A Graded Series of Bible Class Literature

Primary
Year 1 – Books 1-4

Written By

Donna Fowler
Pat Lovelady
Kathleen Johnson

Edited by
Mike Willis and Earl E. Robertson

Associate Editor
Shirley Mohon

Artwork by
Brenda Preuett

ISBN 10: 1-58427-3623

ISBN 13: 978-1-58427-3622

truth
BOOKS

Guardian of Truth Foundation
CEI Bookstore
220 S. Marion St.
Athens, AL 35611
1-855-49-BOOKS or 1-855-492-6657
www.truthbooks.net

walking
with GOD

A Graded Series of Bible Class Literature

Primary
Year 1 — Books 1-4

Written By

Donna Fowler
Pat Lovelady
Kathleen Johnson

Edited By
Mike Willis and Earl E. Robertson

Associate Editor
Shirley Mohon

Artwork By
Brenda Preuett

How To Use This Manual

Each lesson in this manual is composed of lesson aims, a pre-class activity, a review session, reinforcing activities, and class worksheets. For each lesson the scripture is given and also a memory verse is recommended. Children from ages six to eight are good at memorizing.

Lesson aims or objectives to be accomplished by each lesson are listed. Keep these in mind in preparing and teaching. Evaluate your lesson to determine if you accomplished these.

The *pre-class activities* are designed to be used the first few minutes after the children enter the room until the actual class begins. These activities can be a form of review, an introduction or interest for the lesson of the hour, or an activity to meet another objective for the class.

Use the *review session* to go over the last lesson or lessons up to this point. This will help the child develop some continuity.

The *approach to the lesson* should arouse the childs interest. When relating the lesson to the children, be enthusiastic and use expression, examples familiar to them, and visual aids to make it more interesting. Involve the students as much as possible. Explain how the lesson applies to them and their everyday living. It may be more appropriate to pray in the lesson section of the class rather than having a set time each class. You might also elect to begin or end each class with a prayer.

The *reinforcing activity* is a repetition of the lesson in another form Repetition helps them to remember the main points.

The *student worksheets* have been designed for the teacher to use as homework, a quiz in class, a study guide for however he sees best. The *questions* or *exercises* in the student book should also be checked or reviewed. Encourage the students to study their lessons and complete the exercises in their books before class. For the older or advanced students you may elect to give them extra assignments to challenge their minds and add depth to the lesson.

The student book also contains an *evaluation sheet* which has proven to benefit the teacher, student and the parents.

Table Of Contents

Important Information For The Teacher

You, as a Bible class teacher, play an important part in the child's life. In addition to teaching him the Scriptures, you will be helping him to become a person, to learn to give and take, and to get along with his fellow classmates. Because of this, you need to understand as much about the elementary age child as possible. You can read books pertaining to the age level you are teaching and also observe this age child at play to gain a better knowledge of why they are the way they are and gain insight how to better handle classroom situations which you will encounter. When a child plays, he exposes his inner self, home life, and any problems that he may have. Hopefully, you will not need to spend as much time in explaining acceptable behavior and class routines expected of the child as was needed when he was younger.

Children this age have good active minds and are able and eager to learn facts and memorize. They may become easily bored and act as troublemakers if the teacher is not prepared to guide and answer their many questions. Therefore, the teacher of this age child must be enthusiastic, eager, pleasant, interesting, and interested in the children and their problems. This age child is very perceptive and sensitive to others and his surroundings. He likes to compete and wants to win. They need to be challenged and their energy needs to be channeled in the right direction. They thrive on praise for their efforts.

All children like to learn; this makes them feel important. They have a natural curiosity that gives them pleasure when it is satisfied. Children need to use their growing abilities to accomplish various tasks. Each child is different from all others. No two children grow or develop in exactly the same way; therefore, all of the children in your class will not and should not be expected to do all of the things equally well.

The preschool child has associated mainly with his family; but now he begins to branch out with other children and in group activities as he begins schools. The six-year-old is gradually settling down. He is not as carefree as he appears; by observing his play and his talking to friends, you will discover some of his worries, fears, and views about life. He is not always sure he is loved and is often jealous of others, he constantly needs reassurance. He likes for things to stay familiar. This is demonstrated by the fact that he loves the same story over and over again. Acceptance and accomplishment are most important to him. As the child enters school, he already knows the sound and meaning of many words. He cannot write, but he does enjoy drawing pictures, and, occasionally, you can get him to interpret them.

The six-year-old does not retain his moods for a long period of time. He fluctuates between periods of being loud and high spirited to periods of pensive thinking. By the time he is six, he should have learned to obey, have self-control, and be self-reliant. He accepts the teacher as the authority and does not question this role. Physically, he is very active but tires easy. He is also clumsy, self-centered, and a bit sloppy. His attention span is approximately ten to fifteen minutes. Because of this, the teacher must alternate between quiet activities and those that require action.

The seven-year-old is maturing and is more conscious of others' feelings. His eye and hand coordination is better than a year ago. He is not growing as fast as he did at six. The seven-year-old still searches for a friend as does the six-year-old. He feels the pressure of his home and school life. He wants to please and satisfy but the burden is there.

At seven or eight, he questions the authority of his teacher. He may do annoying things to distract the teacher. He may annoy his neighbor, wave his hand when he has nothing to say, etc. Part of his behavior is simply to get attention and part of it is to test the teacher to see what the teacher will do to him. The seven-year-old often resorts to name-calling as a defense mechanism when playing with other children. This has become a problem in some Bible classes; often the teacher must handle this situation. Make the child aware that he is hurting others' feelings and ask him if God would want him to hurt others or would he like to be called by the name which he is calling his friend. He also likes to tell tall tales. He reflects his emotional need to be strong, brave, free, independent, and powerful.

The eight-year-old often regards the six and seven-year-olds as babies. The eight-year-old is more mature. He is most sensitive to peer pressure and criticism. He strives to be like the others in dress and actions. He can read well and is writing now. He likes to help and is most capable. He likes to impart his knowledge to the younger students and help teach them. He is good at using his hands to make things and work with such materials as cardboard, pencils, pens, scissors, glue, glitter, clay, tape, etc. He enjoys role-playing, storytelling, pictures, crafts, and objects to handle.

Remember that all children like security, love, control, faith, guidance, independence, protection, and acceptance.

The Creation
Genesis 1-2

Lesson Aims

1. To teach the students that God created the world and to arouse a deep feeling of respect for God as the Creator.

2. To point out the basic theory of evolution and that it contradicts what God has revealed.

3. To teach a basic understanding of the Godhead and the fact that all were present at the creation.

Pre-Class Activity

1. As the children enter the room, each could place a moon on their attendance charts. The charts could be simply made to look like any open window would look as you gaze through it from inside your home. At each following lesson a new star could be added to show the child's participation in each class. Gummed stars and moon could be used or ones made from different colored pieces of construction paper (pre-cut before class).

2. On a table you could have some beautiful pictures (cut from a magazine and mounted on construction paper) representing each day of creation. The children could look through them and pick out their favorite one. Each child can tell briefly why this is their favorite. These same pictures can be used to review at the next class meeting.

Review Session

1. This time might be used to discuss objectives or class discipline.

2. Perhaps the class might plan an outing some Saturday during this series of lessons to a park where all of God's creation might be observed or to a zoo to reinforce the lesson on Noah.

Approach To The Lesson

1. Prior to the class find a picture of a man. Mount the picture on a piece of construction paper and cut it up into 4 or 5 pieces, making a human puzzle. Blindfold one of the children with a handkerchief and give him the first piece to be tacked on the bulletin board. This will resemble somewhat the game of pin-the-tail-on-the-donkey. Continue this until all the pieces are on the board. You could then point out that in order to make a man, it takes someone who (1) can see, (2) has the intelligence to do it, and (3) is much more intelligent than we. You can also point out that God's book tells us the *truth* about where we came from. The other "stories" they might hear are only some man's ideas to try to explain away God.

2. You could have a globe on a small table with a high intensity light shining on it. (The curtains could be drawn and the lights out for an even greater effect.) You could walk over to the table and say something like "Have you ever wondered how our earth was made? Some people think it came from nowhere, but let's see what God's word tells us about the creation of the world."

The Lesson: Points To Emphasize

1. The wonderful way in which God made things: by merely speaking, and it was so.

2. That everything He made was good — the beauty of the world.

3. That the *Bible* is true and other "stories" are in fact just that — stories which men made up.

4. Third day: You could point out here that from this point on, the full-grown trees had the seed to reproduce after their own kind. A brief explanation that God's plan has been from the beginning that each produces after its own kind. This will confirm your previous point on the error of evolution.

5. Sixth day: Explain in simple terms the Godhead, from the statement, "Let *us* make man in our own image."

Reinforcing Activities

1. Creation Game. In the center of a bulletin board have a circle with the numbers 1-7. Have a large headed pin or tack with a short string tied to it pinned at each number. Surrounding the circle have 7 pictures each representing one day of creation. Have the children come up, one at a time and match the string with the appropriate picture.

2. Memory Verse. Print the memory verse on construction paper and cut it up into phrases. Pass the cards around the room and let each child select a phrase. Ask the child with the first part of the verse to come pin it to the bulletin board. Then, see if the others can each add their part until the verse is complete. Ask the class to say the verse in unison with you. Any child who knows the verse before this activity should be encouraged to say the verse before the class and given the appropriate praise for doing so. Upon completion of this exercise all the children should know the memory verse.

3. Song: "How Great Thou Art." This song could be more effectively taught if you will try to find pictures from a magazine to illustrate the phrases of the song. "Oh Lord my God, when I in awesome wonder" (a picture of a child gazing out a window), "Consider all the worlds thy hands have made" (have a picture of earth or planets, etc.). Do this with at least the first verse and chorus of the song. You might, time and finances permitting, mount the pictures on construction paper and place them in a spiral bound photo album. The words could be printed or typed next to the pictures. As you teach the song, hold the book with the pictures and words out in front of you so that they can see the very words which they are singing visualized in front of them. This book will be very durable and can be used for years to come as an aid for future Bible classes.

Application

At this point, you could stress that the creation narrative tells us that we were created in God's own image. We were not created from a monkey, as the theory of evolution suggests. We all have a certain amount of creativity in us and should use our talents to serve God and reflect his image.

(See bulletin boards for visual reinforcement of application.)

Visual Displays

Evolution Monkeys

With God's Word

Let Us Make Man In Our Image

1. Obey parents.
2. Choose friends carefully.
3. Study God's word.
4. Attend worship.
5. Pray daily.

In-Class Worksheet

You may use these sheets as reinforcement of lesson. It may be advantageous to use them as a quiz as this would help you measure your effectiveness as a teacher. Another possibility would be to collect them after each class and present the students with a notebook of all the worksheets at the conclusion of these lessons.

The First Home
(Genesis 2-4:2)

Lesson Aims

1. The student will be able to state the structure of the home: God as the head of Christ, Christ as the head of man, man as the head of woman, children to obey parents.

2. The student will realize how subtle sin can be and be made aware that no bells ring or lights flash when sin is committed. Only a study of God's word can reveal what is pleasing to God.

Pre-Class Activity

1. Place star on attendance chart.

2. On an activity table, try to create a "mini" Garden of Eden. Have some beautiful potted plants and a very "tempting" bowl of delicious fruit. A small rubber snake could be purchased from the variety store and placed near the forbidden fruit. If potted plants or artificial ones are not available, you could make a shoe box scene with dirt and small plants from your yard. You could let the children *look* at the fruit, but remind them that it is forbidden; they may not eat it or touch it. The rubber snake might spark some reaction from which you could talk of why the snake is so hated by man. You might also point out that the fruit could have been like an apple, but we do not know the exact kind of fruit which tempted Adam and Eve.

Review Session

Using the cards you made from the previous lesson, hold them up and ask the children which day of creation God made the item on the card. Question why evolution is wrong (see if anyone can quote memory verse from last class as an answer to this question). Ask if anyone can tell who else was present at the creation with God.

Approach To The Lesson

1. You could ask a question like, "Have you ever had to move from a home where you were very happy? Today's lesson tells how the first man and woman were forced to leave their beautiful home because they disobeyed God."

2. Or you might say something like, "Have you ever wondered why your daddy has to leave every morning just so you can have food to eat? God's word tells us why all men have to work by the sweat of their brows. It wasn't always that way."

Lesson: Points To Emphasize

1. God provided everything Adam and Eve could have possibly wanted or needed.

2. Satan did not point out the bad things that would happen to Eve but tricked her into thinking that her actions were acceptable.

2

3. Adam and Eve were punished for their sin, as was the snake. Sin brings unhappiness, punishment and death.

4. They would have remained happy if they had obeyed God. They made an incorrect choice.

5. God has a plan that, if we obey Him, He has promised to let us live with Him when we die.

Reinforcing Activities

1. *Praying*. Prayer that would reinforce the lesson might include:
   a. Praying for God to help us choose the things that will make Him happy by not being deceived by sin as was Eve.
   b. Thanking God for the opportunity to work for our food, clothing and homes in spite of our sins.
   c. Asking God for help to obey our parents, remembering that Adam and Eve disobeyed God, their Father and Creator.

2. *Role Playing*. Let the children act out the lesson. You can let the child who is acting as Satan hold the rubber snake from the activity table and offer a piece of fruit to Eve. Instruct the children not to really take a bite of the fruit. You might bring towels to use as animal skins for when the Lord clothed Adam and Eve.

3. *Film Strip*. Be sure to preview any visual aid of this type for accuracy and relevancy.

4. *Singing*. Sing "Trust and Obey" while using a picture song book. See the first lesson for details on how to make a picture song book to help the children visualize the words to the adult songs.

5. *Memory Verse*. See lesson one for instructions of the game to help all in the class to learn memory verses. Be sure to explain the memory verses to the children so they understand the impact of them and not simply memorize meaningless words.

Application

1. Adam and Eve made an incorrect choice. They were deceived by sin. These children will soon be making choice about whether to serve God or to go the way of the world. Some have already tasted liquor or smoked a cigarette. In a kindergarten class surveyed recently, more than half the children had either smoked or drank or both, usually encouraged by their parents! How frightful to think of parents so out of tune with God's word that they think it "cute" to offer these killers to precious children! (See bulletin board for visual reinforcement against drinking, smoking and drugs.) Ask the children, while pointing to the first picture on the board, if they know of anyone (perhaps in their class in school) who brags about smoking, drinking and drugs. Warn them of drug pushers. Their own classmates may even try to make them feel like an outcast because they refuse to participate. Emphasize the fact that God's people would avoid sin even though most people in the world appear to approve such actions.

2. Explain to the children God's plan for the home. See bulletin board number two. If they obey their parents, they are pleasing to God. In using pictures to display bulletin board number two, be sure to use something as clouds for God and perhaps a cross for Jesus. It is best not to use actual pictures of people to represent deity.

Visual Displays

Bulletin Board One: "Do Not Be Tricked By Sin"

Draw:
1. For tobacco — a pack of cigarettes.
2. For alcohol — a bottle of liquor.
3. For drugs — a bottle of pills.

Bulletin Board Two: "Children Obey Your Parents."

(In-Class Worksheet)

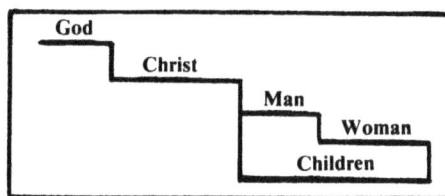

1. Crossword Answers:

Down: 1. Death 3. Leave 5. Sin   6. Eve
Across: 3. Lied   2. Adam   4. Eden   5. Snake.

2. Poem Answers:

a. Eden   b. tree or fruit   c. sun   d. Adam or man
e. sin.

3

The First Brothers
(Genesis 4:1-15, 25, 26)

Lesson Aims

1. To show the student the necessity of following God's word exactly and to warn against doctines of men.

2. To acquaint the student with the patriarchal method of offering animal sacrifice as worship to God.

3. To teach that sorrow is always the result of sin.

4. To show how sibling rivalry can cause much heartache in the home.

Pre-Class Activity

1. Place a star on attendance chart.

2. You can build an altar (or let the children help you build it) to resemble the kind Cain and Abel might have used. This can be done by using cardboard blocks or bricks. You can made homemade bricks by collecting cigar boxes and covering them with adhesive paper that resembles block or stone. A small stuffed lamb could be placed on the altar along with some sticks to represent kindling. If it is not practical to build a large altar, you could gather some stones and build a small replica on a small table. The sacrificial lamb could then come from any child's barnyard set.

As the children enter the room you could stress how important it is that we do exactly what God commands.

This would also be a good time to explain that we are not told to offer animal sacrifices today because Jesus was our sacrifice. Before Jesus came, worship to God was much different than it is now. You could also have an open Bible on the table with a marker between the Old and New Testament; explain that our lesson today comes from the Old Testament and that was before Jesus came.

Review Session

You can read the poem from the "In Class Worksheet" (from the previous lesson) and see if the children can still fill in the blanks correctly. Question them to see if they can explain the structure of the home.

Approach To The Lesson

1. Riddle: "I was Adam and Eve's first son and might have brought them much joy, only I became jealous of my brother and in anger I killed him. Who am I?"

2. Question: "Have you ever been so jealous or angry with your brother or sister that you really wished they had never been born? We all have probably had bad feelings like that at some time or another. Today our lesson is about the first two brothers. Unfortunately the oldest brother, Cain, did not learn to control his feelings and when he became angry with his brother Abel, he killed him. This is the way it happened."

Lesson: Points To Emphasize

1. During the Patriarchal Age, God required a "blood" sacrifice of an unblemished animal. Cain's offering had no blood and this was very displeasing to God.

2. Cain was selfish. He wanted things done his way or not at all. He disobeyed God. He chose to trust his own thoughts rather than what he knew God had commanded.

3. Cain should not have been angry because Abel did right.

4. Cain brought great sorrow upon his mother and father. He took the life of Abel and then, as punishment, he was banished from where they lived. The family was unhappy because one son did not do right.

Reinforcing Activities

1. *Finger Playing:*

Cain and Abel were brothers. (hold up index fingers)

Both made an offering to God. (spread hands palms up)

But Cain's offering was bad. (thumbs down)

God would not accept it. (shake head no)

Cain was very angry. (make a fist)

He killed Abel. (raise hand as if to strike with knife)

God punished Cain. (shake finger)

He had to leave. (make fingers walk away)

His mother and dad were very sad. (wipe tears from cheek)

2. *Role Playing.* Let the children act out the lesson. This is always an excellent reinforcement as children tend to remember 90% of what they do and very little of what they only hear. You could use a child's toy rubber knife for the weapon and the toy lamb for the acceptable sacrifice. If you have made a large altar as suggested in the pre-class activity, that could also be used along with some artificial fruit to complete the scene for the children. Any excess children could be lambs in Abel's herd witnessing the murder.

3. *Singing.* Sing "Trust and Obey." Using the picture song book from the previous lesson, stress that Abel did trust and obey God. Even though he was killed, we know that he will be rewarded for his obedience. Cain did not trust God enough to obey Him but thought he could improve on God's commandment. He was punished.

4. *Memory Verse.* See lesson one for instructions of the game to help all in the class learn the memory verse. Be sure to discuss its meaning with the class.

Application

1. Cain did not act acceptably. He tried to improve God's law. Then jealousy provoked him to commit murder. Jealousy and other bad feelings are present in all of us from time to time. If the children realize that, with God's help, they can learn to control these feelings and, in controlling them, can overcome them, then our lesson will have been effective. Stress the good feelings that come from serving God. See bulletin board and worksheet for reinforcement of this idea.

2. Beware of commandments of men. Stress how easy it is for error to creep in when men try to improve on God's

commandments. Men try to do the same thing today that incriminated Cain. We must study God's word to find the way He wants us to worship and we should exclude any practice that is not found therein.

Visual Displays

Bulletin Board.

Unacceptable		Acceptable
Lying		Truth
Jealousy		Love
Hate		Obedience
Rebellion		Faith
Doubt		

In-Class Worsheet

1. *Scripture Drill.* These fill-in-the-blank verses are intended to reinforce the lesson. Matt. 7:21 shows us that like Cain those who try to change God's will and worship in their own way will not enter God's kingdom. Gal. 5:22-23 shows that when we are Christians and study God's word, bad feelings (Cain's anger and jealousy) are replaced by good feelings and peace.

The Flood
(Genesis 6:13-9:19)

Lesson Aims

1. To show the student God's love and care for all who love and obey him.

2. To show that God expects us to do right even when those about us are doing wrong.

3. To develop in each child a deep faith and trust in God like that of Noah.

Pre-Class Activity

1. Place a star on attendance chart.

2. In the center of a table have an empty washtub with a small toy boat in the center. As the children enter the room, let each child take a turn at adding about one glassful of water until the boat begins to float. You can ask the children if anyone can tell you about a time in Bible history when a very large boat saved the only righteous people on the entire earth from a terrible flood. You will be able to tell those who have studied their lessons by the spirited response you will get.

3. Collect the pictures the children have brought in from home. Paste them to construction paper to use for the review at the next class meeting.

Review Session

1. Make flash cards with the words Cain, Abel, sacrifice, altar, murderer, shepherd, and farmer. Hold the cards up one at a time to see if the children can tell you a little bit about each one.

2. Question the class to see if anyone can explain the patriarchal method of offering animal sacrifice.

An Approach To The Lesson

1. You could start your lesson with a statement such as, "Have you ever wondered why we see a rainbow so often after a rain? That rainbow is the sign of God's promise that He will never destroy the earth by flood again. Today's lesson is about the time God did destroy the earth by flood. This is the way it happened."

2. You could pick up the toy boat used in the pre-class activity and ask if anyone in the class has ever been on a boat out in the ocean so far that they could not see any land at all. Then compare that situation with Noah who had no land to go to. He was in the ark over one year and knew only that God was guiding him and his family.

Lesson: Points To Emphasize

1. After Cain killed Abel the people of the world were filled with wickedness. Satan dominated the lives of all the people except eight, Noah and his family.

2. Noah followed God's command exactly in building

5

the ark. He also preached to the people for 120 years. During that time, God gave the wicked people plenty of time to repent.

3. When the people rejected Noah's preaching, they were really rejecting God.

5. God used the same water to save Noah and his family that he used to destroy the wicked.

6. When the land was once again dry, Noah and his family had been inside the ark for over one year. The first thing they did was to offer sacrifice and worship God. When we are thankful for God's blessings, we should always remember to pray and thank God.

7. God promised never to destroy the earth again by flood, and as a sign of this covenant He placed the rainbow in the sky.

Reinforcing Activities

1. *Praying:* In offering a prayer to God, ask God to give us faith like Noah so that we will do right even when others around us are doing wrong.

2. *Singing:* Sing "Trust and Obey" using the picture song book from the previous lesson. You can emphasize how much Noah had to both trust and obey God. If time permits, you could also sing "How Great Thou Art" using the picture song book from lesson one. Emphasize here that God had the power not only to create the world but also to destroy it at His will.

3. *Role Playing:* You can try to find a large cardboard box which can act as your ark. A small child's workbench with hammer and pegs could represent the actual building of the ark. Be sure to have Noah preach about the forthcoming doom as he steadily hammers away. Some small stuffed animals could be carried by any children playing animals. Let as many as will actually fit, climb inside the box while the others can act like they are crying, realizing their doom. Any small branch from your yard will act nicely as an olive branch and the altar stones from the previous lesson can be used to illustrate Noah offering sacrifices and worshiping God after leaving the ark. Stress to the children that even though they are pretending, that these events really happened.

4. *Bulletin Board.* You could make Noah's Ark riding on the water. A storm cloud (black with lightning) could be added as you tell that part of the lesson. When the rain stops you could take down the storm cloud and put in its place a large yellow sun. Also you could make a mountain to insert between the water and the ark. Building a bulletin board as you tell the lesson is a valuable way of presenting your lesson.

Applications

1. *God keeps His promises:* The children should realize some of God's promises, and the fact that He will keep all those promises. See bulletin board number one under Visual Displays for further application. Stress to the children that God cares for us and loves us. Try to develop a strong faith inside each one of them so they *know* that God will indeed keep His promises.

2. *God will bless those who serve Him:* Noah and his family were spared from a terrible death because they loved and obeyed God. Discuss some of the ways God has blessed us; providing homes, fathers, mothers, food, friends, teachers, and beautiful world in which to live.

Visual Displays

In-Class Worksheet

1. *Scripture Drill:* Have the children look up the scriptures listed and help them fill in the appropriate spaces. Discuss with them how these scriptures also relate to the lesson.

2. *True or False.* Answers: 1. False; 2. False; 3. True; 4. True; 5. False.

3. *Noah Word Search.* Answers: 1. Ark; 2. Animals; 3. Faith; 4. Rainbow; 5. Flood; 6. Rain; 7. Love; 8. Dove.

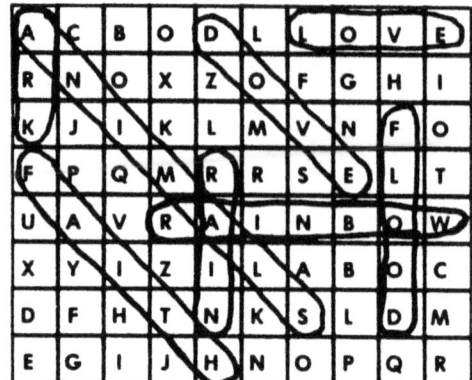

The Tower of Babel
(Genesis 11:1-9)

Lesson Aims

1. To show that man can not stand alone. No man or group of men can ever accomplish anything that is not God's will.

2. To show that it is only through prayer and study of God's word that we can humble ourselves in a Christ-like manner to be pleasing to God.

3. To show that we are not to exalt ourselves but rather to humble ourselves to be pleasing to God.

Pre-class Activity

1. Have each child place a star on his attendance chart.

2. As the children enter the room you might greet them with "Buenos Dias" which is Spanish for "Good Day." You could also check some books on foreign languages and try to say some simple phrases in several different languages such as "Bonjour" (bohng-zhoor), which is "hello" in French. Use just enough to arouse their curiosity. Ask the children if any of them have ever visited a country where any other language was spoken, or if any of them can speak a different language? You could have some encyclopedias on a table opened to foreign countries. Ask the children if they know why there are so many different languages? Tell them our lesson today explains how all these different languages came about.

3. Discuss some of the differences and similarities of people who speak a language different than ours.

Review Session

1. Hold up the pictures that the children brought to class from the last meeting and review the lesson on Noah. You may have to add a few pictures to round out the review.

2. You might ask a question like, "What do you think of when you see a rainbow?"

Approach To The Lesson

1. Consult a Bible Handbook for pictures of the ruins of towers thought to be similar to the tower of Babel. Stress that no one is certain of its location but there is strong evidence to indicate that one structure might be like the ruins. It is always very effective to show pictures of ruins which reinforces the fact that what God deems wrong will not flourish. You can go from this discussion right into the lesson.

2. There is a painting which is an artist's interpretation of what the tower of Babel might have looked like that can be found in most large family Bibles. There is also a transparency of this painting in the Milliken series that can be used with an overhead projector. You can show this to the children and explain that this is the type of tower that

would have been built in those days. Then proceed to tell the lesson.

The Lesson: Points To Emphasize

1. The people's hearts were wicked; they wanted to build a tower *to make a great name for themselves* and *exalt themselves as gods*. They also did not want to be scattered over the earth.

2. God saw this as the beginning of a terrible rebellion. He separated them by confusing their language. The people were naturally dispersed over the face of the earth. The tower was never finished.

3. The people sinned when they thought they could do anything they wanted to do without God's help.

4. Many people are still the same as those who tried to build the tower and we must be different from them. We can show God how much we love Him by obeying His will, and trusting Him to do what is best for us.

Reinforcing Activities

1. *Poem Game.* Print on cards or construction paper the words German, French, Greek, Russian, Sections, and Best. Tape these papers underneath the children's chairs. Make sure these chairs are filled first. On a bulletin board or blackboard have the following poem printed with the appropriate words missing. At the appropriate time, let the children check underneath their chairs and come up to fill in the missing word.

A great tower we were building to make ourselves great,
But God had in mind for us a different fate.
You would not believe what happened that day
We could not understand the words people would say.
One man spoke English; his name was Herman.
But his boss gave directions to him in _____.
One man we saw just sat on the bench
He spoke Spanish and can't understand _____.
Another man almost fell in the creek
When someone gave him directions in _____.
Another man sat by a pile of stones he was crushin'
As he spoke Hebrew and not _____.
The tower was not ever finished you see with all these languages
It was as confusing as could be.
So we all left in different directions
And by our language divided the world into _____.
Some went, North, South, East, and West
With those people they could understand _____.

2. *Singing.* Sing "Take Time To Be Holy." This song could be more effectively taught by making a picture song book. (See lesson 1 for instructions.)

3. *Memory Verse.* The memory verse could possibly be taught with the song as the two thoughts coincide.

4. *Role Playing.* Remember, children remember so much more if they are allowed to participate. For this reason, role playing is a very effective reinforcement. Do not worry that they will get tired of this activity; they love it.

5. *Praying.* At a convenient time in your lesson have one of the children word a prayer. You might ask them to be sure to ask God to let us always give Him the honor and glory and not to be like those who built the tower of Babel.

Application

The people who built the tower of Babel failed to glorify God. They wanted to make themselves great. We must be sure that all that we do is for God's glory. See visual display for reinforcement of application.

Visual Displays

1. Bulletin Board.

2. Bulletin Board or Flannel Graph.

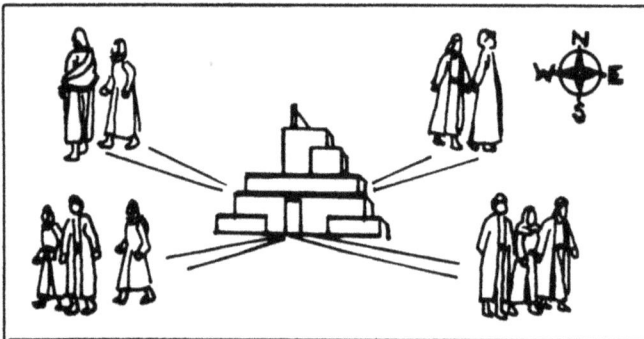

In-Class Worksheet

Scripture Drill. (Psa. 37:23-27). Help the children fill in the blanks and explain each verse to them. Help them appreciate that God will take care of us if we will only walk in His way.

Abraham: An Unselfish Uncle
(Genesis 12:1-9; 13:1-13)

Lesson Aims

1. To teach that it was through Abraham's descendants that the nation of Israel and Christ were born, stressing the importance of keeping the lineage pure.

2. To teach that God wants us to be unselfish as was Abraham.

Pre-class Activity

1. Have each child place a star on their attendance chart.

2. On a table have several all-occasion cards. As the children enter the room, you could have each one pick out one of the cards. Explain what each one expresses. A birthday card expresses love and joy toward a friend. You are telling him you are glad he or she was born. A sympathy card expresses love and sorrow for a friend because they have just lost someone they loved very much. Teach the children the joy of unselfishly sharing the joys and sorrows of those they love. They will learn to appreciate those acts of kindness shown by their friends when they receive a card from them. Encourage the class to send one of the appropriate cards to a shut-in. Have them each sign their name. You may have to help some of the first graders. Then mail it for them. If someone in your congregation has just had a baby, you might also want to send an appropriate card. You could also discuss other acts of kindness such as visiting the sick, taking a small bouquet of flowers, calling a shut-in on the telephone (circumstances permitting) to tell them that they are missed, etc. Stress to the children that we pray to God and ask His protection for those who are sick, trusing that no matter what happens it will be the very best for the person involved.

Review Session

Following the pre-class activity in which you have stressed being unselfish and trying to encourage others, a few simple questions would be a good introduction to a short review of the last lesson.

1. How were the people who built the Tower of Babel selfish?

2. What did God do to stop them from finishing the tower?

3. Does God feel that we are better than other people because we speak English and live differently than people do in other countries?

Approach To The Lesson

1. "Do you remember the people in the last lesson who did not trust and obey God? Let's sing "Trust and Obey" to remind us of what we should do." Sing "Trust and Obey" using the picture song book. Our lesson today is

about one man who did trust and obey God and many times had to do things that were very difficult to do. Everytime he put his life in the hands of God, He took care of him. Proceed to tell today's lesson.

2. The use of a riddle is always interesting to the children. You might say something like, "I am thinking of a Bible hero who, when he was already very old, was told by God to leave his country and journey to a far away land. He trusted God and obeyed him. Who was he?"

The Lesson: Points To Emphasize

1. After God had scattered the people, the earth again became very sinful.

2. God chose Abraham because he, like Noah, was trying to please God. This was unusual because most of the people around him had turned to sinful idol worship.

3. God told Abraham, "Get thee out of thy country, and from thy kindred and from thy father's house, into a land that I will show thee . . ." God promised that through Abraham's descendants Jesus would be born.

4. Abraham was seventy-five years old when he left Ur. Lot went with him.

5. God blessed Abraham. He was very rich in livestock, silver, and gold. Lot also had many possessions.

6. Lot's herdsmen and Abraham's herdsmen began arguing over grazing rights because of their large herds. They agreed to separate.

7. Abraham was unselfish. He let Lot choose first which way he wanted to go. Lot was selfish and chose the well-watered valley of the Jordan. That left Abraham with the less desirable land.

Reinforcing Activities

1. *Pantomime Story.* Have the children repeat each fingerplay and say the words following each phrase. Then repeat the story, doing only the actions, and let the children tell you what part of the lesson it represents.

> God chose Abraham. (Put hand over eyes as if looking for Abraham. Point as if you have found him.)
> Because Abraham loved God. (Put hand on heart.)
> God promised to bless Abraham. (Hold both arms out as if arms are too full to carry all the blessings.)
> Abraham had to leave his home. (Let your fingers walk.)
> To a far land God would show him. (Look up as to look far away shielding eyes as if from sun.)
> Lot's men and Abraham's men started to argue. (Shake fist.)
> Abraham said, "Let's not fight." (Shake head no.)
> If you go left. (Look to the left.)
> I will go right. (Look to the right.)

2. *Singing.* Sing "Take Time To Be Holy" using picture song book from last week's lesson.

3. *Praying.* In the prayer, ask God to help the children learn to be unselfish as was Abraham. You might find some pictures representing things they might tend to be selfish about — toys, friends, food and pets. Paste these on a large sheet of construction paper and write a simple prayer in words they can understand. After showing it to them and discussing the various items ask one of the children to say a prayer.

4. *Memory Verse.* Teach the memory verse by using the memory verse game or any other method you have found successful.

Application

1. God chose Abraham, an unselfish man, to become the father of the nation of Israel. God promised him land, and numberless children. These promises were fulfilled in the formation of the nation of Israel and Israel conquering the land of Caanan. These were wonerful promises. Abraham knew he would have a large family and much land and wealth to leave them. It was comforting to know that he would be so blessed by God taking care of his family so richly.

There was a third promise made to Abraham that through his family all nations of the earth would be blessed! This was saying that Jesus would be born through Abraham's family and that only through Christ could all nations have the hope of eternal blessings. Through Jesus we have come to know God and His will for us more perfectly. Through Jesus, God has provided a way that we can live with Him after we die. (See bulletin board for visual display.)

2. Abraham was unselfish. God wants us to be unselfish. Everything we have is God's and we should always be willing to take "the lesser" and give "the more." You could help the children see that by giving they are actually receiving a dual blessing. Firstly, they have made someone else happy by being generous to them. Secondly, they have pleased God by humbling themselves.

Visual Displays
Bulletin Board

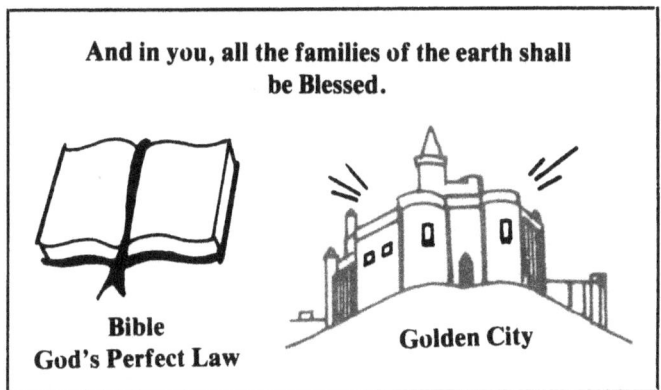

And in you, all the families of the earth shall be Blessed.

Bible
God's Perfect Law

Golden City

In-Class Worksheets

Answers to crossword:

Down	Across
1. Drink	5. Obeyed
2. Lot	6. Visit
3. Better	7. Abraham
4. Feed	

Abraham And Issac
(Genesis 21:1-7, 22:1-18, 26:12-22)

Lesson Aims

1. To teach the children the benefit of enduring tests; that it strengthens our faith in God and we become stronger for having had the experience. Also, stress that trials do not last forever. We should look toward the future with hope.

2. To teach the children to encouarge their parents in times of stress.

3. To teach the children that God watches over us at all times, even in times of stress.

4. To teach that Issac's love for God was a direct result of Abraham's example.

Pre-class Activity

1. Have each child add a star on their attendance chart.

2. Before class you could make a cardboard figure of Abraham offering Issac. This could be done by tracing a picture of the event (see visual display) on a blank transparency. Place the transparency on an overhead projector and shine it on a bulletin board. Tack several pieces of paper on the bulletin board until the proper size is reached. Now trace the image on the paper that is being projected from the transparency. After you make your pattern you can glue the paper with the picture of Abraham offering Isaac to a piece of cardboard. Cut it out with a cardboard knife and color with markers. Cut off Abraham's arm at the elbow with the knive in it and replace with a brad. This enables the arm to swing down as if he were going to kill Issac. Have the figure leaning against a large table and as the children come in you could ask them if they know who this figure represents. Encourage them to move the arm up and down. Ask the children if they can tell you whether or not Abraham had to really offer Issac. This will give you a good indication as to whether or not they have studied their lesson. You could also make a small thicket by bringing in some small branches and having a small stuffed animal with its head caught in it. These could all be used as props at the time when the children play act the lesson.

Review Session

Walk over to your cardboard Abraham and ask the children "Does this man seem like the unselfish uncle we studied about last week?" Then ask some pertinent questions as the following:

1. Can anyone remember his name?
2. How did Abraham show he was unselfish?
3. What did God promise Abraham?

An Approach To The Lesson

1. You could ask a question like, "Have you ever had to do something that was really hard for you to do? Maybe your parents told you to do something and you knew they must be right, but the fact that it was the right thing to do did not make it any easier. Our lesson today is about a man who was told by God to offer up his only son as a sacrifice. He knew it was the right thing to do, to obey God, but *oh* how his heart must have ached inside!"

2. You could approach the lesson by telling a story: "Jim's parents had just bought him a new bicycle. Jim had waited a very long time for the bike and was very proud when he rode it.

"After a short time had passed, some friends of Jim's family had a tragedy. Their daddy had been hurt in an accident and would not be able to work for a very long time. The oldest boy had a chance to get a paper route to help earn some money, but he did not have a bike to deliver the papers.

"Jim's parents told him to give his bike to his friend. Jim knew it was the right thing to do, but *oh*, how he would miss the bicycle. It was a very hard thing for him to do.

"Our lesson today is about a man who was told by God to do a very hard thing. This is the way it happened."

The Lesson: Points To Emphasize

1. Issac was the fulfillment of a promise God made to Abraham.

2. God told Abraham to sacrifice Issac.

3. Abraham loved and trusted God enough to obey any command.

4. God saw Abraham's faith and did not let him actually harm Issac.

5. Issac, when grown would rather give up the wells than have trouble.

6. Issac was happier and received greater blessing because he loved peace rather than quarrelling and fighting.

Reinforcing Activities

1. *Praying.* You could lead the class in a fervent prayer making sure to ask God to give us faith and trust in him as did Abraham.

2. *Singing.* Sing "Trust and Obey" emphasizing how much Abraham had to trust God to obey this particular commandment. Use your picture song book as a visual aid to reinforce the song. You might also use "Take Time to be Holy."

3. *Memory Verse.* Using the memory verse game (see lesson one), teach the memory verse. Explain to the children that even in times of trouble, God provides.

4. *Play Acting.* Assign characters to as many of the children as possible. You can write out a little script or just have them ad-lib, whichever you prefer.

Application

1. We all have trying times. The children might have trouble with bullies at school, difficulty with a certain subject at school, poor health, or any number of problems.

You could find pictures in magazines that might represent some of these trials, mount them on construction paper and place them on a bulletin board. (See Visual Displays.) Talk about some of the tests people might endure today.

Be sure to ask the children what trials they might have gone through. Encourage them and help them to realize that the bad times do not last forever. Help them to realize that they can be a big help to their parents when their parents are suffering through a trying time. They can pray about the problem, obey their parents and not cause any more commotion, or it may be a problem that they can actually do something to help in a physical way.

2. Issac grew up to be a peace-loving man. He was a direct result of Abraham's example. We can grow up to be peace loving by patterning ourselves after God's Word. Encourage the children to study their Bibles, and to make heros out of Bible characters.

Visual Displays

Bulletin Board

Model of Abraham offering Issac

11

Jacob and Esau
(Genesis 25:27-34; 27:1-45)

Lesson Aims

1. To teach that kindness and fair dealing brings happiness and that the opposite traits bring unhappiness.

2. To teach the providence of God that, before the boys were born, God told Rebekah, "And the older shall serve the younger." Stress that this information did not give Rebekah the right to lie and manipulate her husband.

Pre-class Activity

1. Have each child place a star on his attendance chart.

2. Have several items on a table that would be familiar to the children. Have some that are fuzzy and some that are smooth (e.g., a stuffed animal, a peach, an apple, and a ball). Take turns blindfolding the children and leading them to the table. Take their hand, barely letting them feel a small portion of the stuffed animal. Then let them barely feel the peach. Both are fuzzy, but can they tell which is which? Now let them smell the animal and the peach. Perhaps now they will have a better idea which is which. Repeat with the apple and the ball. After having this experience the children should be able to relate to Issac when he was being tricked by Jacob.

Review Session

Make flash cards with the words promise, Issac, sacrifice, Moriah, peaceful, and test. Hold them up one at a time and ask the children to tell you how each word related to the previous lesson.

Approach To The Lesson

1. You could stand and take a deep breath and say, "Oh, that food smells so good! I wonder if my brother would give me some. I'm so hungry, I'm about to die." Then proceed to tell the story as if you were Esau.

2. If you could persuade some of the adults to help you, you could act out the lesson of Jacob and Esau.

3. Have your team teacher ask you, "Why are you so sad Rebekah?" Then tell the lesson as if you were Rebekah.

The Lesson: Points To Emphasize

1. God told Rebekah, "Two nations are in thy womb . . and the older shall serve the younger."

2. Jacob's unkindness to his brother was in not giving Esau food.

3. Esau gave up his birthright. He was so worldly that he sold his birthright for a single meal.

4. Selling the birthright meant that Esau would yield to Jacob the head of the family upon the death of their father Issac and lose the larger portion of the inheritance which

was a double portion of his father's estate.

5. Jacob was wrong in deceiving his father. As a result, he suffered much unhappiness. He caused his family to be unhappy and was forced to flee his only brother and leave his family.

6. Rebekah never again saw her beloved son.

7. The entire family suffered because the parents had favorite sons causing the sons not to get along.

Reinforcing Activities

1. *Praying.* Be sure each class period has at least one prayer. Try to pick out a characteristic of the lesson to stress in your prayer.

2. *Singing.* Sing "Take Time to be Holy." Stress that, had Jacob and Esau taken time to be holy, their home could have been much more peaceful.

3. *Memory Verse.* Using the game mentioned in lesson one, teach the memory verse. Discuss it to make sure that the children understand it completely.

4. *Film Strip or Slides.* If you have access to any visual aid (film strip or slides) of this type, it can be an excellent reinforcement of the lesson. Preview it and know what you are going to say. This should never replace preparation for a class but should only be used as a reinforcement of the lesson.

Application

Rebekah and Issac each had a favorite son. The boys did not like each other. What turmoil must have existed in this early home! If the children would learn to appreciate the differences between themselves and their siblings instead of despising them, what a difference could be seen in so many families. Jacob should have given Esau food just because he knew he was hungry. Esau should have thought more of his family responsibility than to sell it for one meal.

Discuss ways families should cooperate with each other. See bulletin board for visual reinforcement of this idea.

Visual Display
A Family is Responsibility and Love

| Daddy Works | Mom Homemaker | Children Go To School | Children Help At Home |

| Baby Needs Help | Family Studying Bible | Children Play | Family Goes To Church |

Jacob's Dream
(Genesis 28:10-22)

Lesson Aids

1. To teach the children that God takes care of us under all circumstances.

2. To encourage the children to give back to God and realize that all belongs to Him.

Pre-class Activity

1. Have each child place a star on their attendance chart.

2. On a table have several pieces of money to include a penny, nickel, dime, quarter, half-dollar, and dollar. As the children enter the room ask them to examine the money and tell you what all those coins have in common. Explain to the children that every coin and all currency printed in the United States has printed on it somewhere "In God We Trust." Talk about ways to spend money that show our trust and faith in God and ways that do not show our trust in God.

Review Session

Write the following sentences on the blackboard and have each child come up and complete them.
1. Issac married R_____.
2. J_____ and E_____ were brothers.
3. E_____ sold his b_____.
4. J_____ tricked I_____ for a blessing.

Approach To The Lesson

1. Ask the children, "Have you ever had a dream that was so real that when you woke up you were still not sure if you were still sleeping?"

2. You could explain that, during the time of Jacob, God sometimes spoke to people in visions and dreams. One of the most beautiful dreams was the one Jacob had.

The Lesson: Points To Emphasize

1. God keeps His promises, He restated the promise to Jacob that He had made to Abraham and Issac.

2. Jacob realized that all of his blessings were from God; hence, he wanted to give back to God a portion of those blessings.

3. Jacob had not always done right, but now he was determined to do right and serve God.

Reinforcing Activities

1. *Dreaming.* Ask the children to close their eyes and pretend they are dreaming. Let God's word tell them of Heaven. This could be accomplished any of several ways. You could possibly read the words of the song "How Beautiful Heaven Must Be", or you might have the song on a casette tape and play it at the appropriate time.

Another way might be to read Rev. 22:1-5. Try to help the children visualize the glory and happiness one will experience in Heaven. Make it such a beautiful picture that each little heart will say to themselves "I want to go to Heaven some day!"

2. *Singing.* Sing "Trust and Obey" to show the children how they might get to Heaven.

3. *Memory Verse.* Teach the memory verse. Have each child tell of a time when they might be afraid, if it were not for the fact that God is with them.

4. *Praying.* Lead a fervent prayer thanking God for His protection, His blessings, and for His promise of a home in Heaven.

Application

Jacob realized that all of his blessings came from God. He promised to give back to God one-tenth of all his blessings. Stress to the children that all of our possessions are gifts from God and we should not count anything as belonging to us, for it is all from God. See bulletin board for visual display. Jacob gave one-tenth. We can give the following:

1. *Money.* Money is needed to buy materials, support preachers, help needy saints, and maintain buildings.

2. *Time.* Stress that giving all the money in the world cannot pay each individual's responsibility to God. He gives us all twenty-four hours in every day. If we do not have time to serve Him, it is because we do not make time.

3. *Homes and Food.* Our homes and food are a gift from God. Sharing our home with someone in need (especially a non-Christian) can show God's love and your love to them. Many have been won to the cause of Christ because of a generous act which opened the door to an individual's heart.

Visual Displays

Bulletin Board

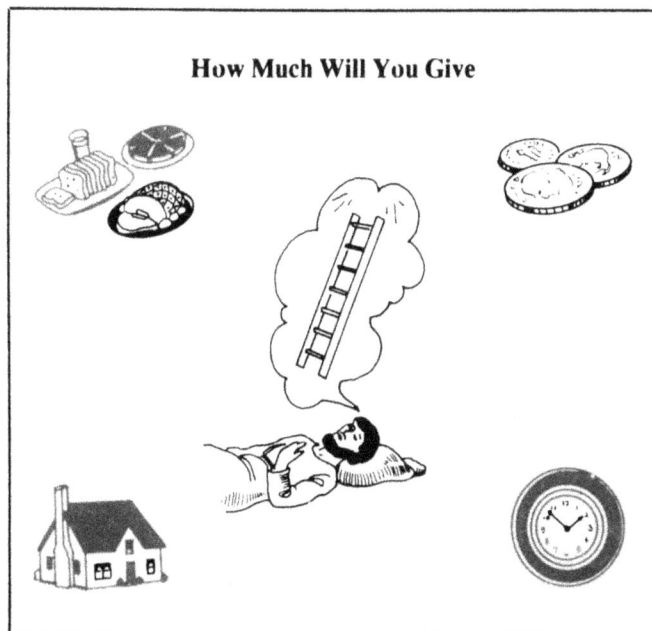

How Much Will You Give

13

Jacob Meets His Brother Again
(Genesis 29:1-20, 31:17-21, 35:23-29)

Lesson Aims

1. To teach that we must do right even though we are not always treated fairly.

2. To impress upon the children the forgiveness demonstrated in the meeting again of Jacob and Esau.

Pre-class Activties

1. Have each child place a star on their attendance chart.

2. Make a sandbox scene of Jacob and Esau meeting. This could be done by using a shoe box (or a larger box if time and materials permit), small animals from a child's barnyard set and popsicle stick figures to represent Jacob and Esau. You could possibly put cotton or steel wool on Esau to make him hairy. Make sure that the sand is deep enough to support the figures.

As the children enter the room you could ask them to gather around the table with your scene. Tell them that this is Jacob and Esau coming together again. Ask them if they can remember what happened to make them separate. Ask them if their brothers had tricked them would they forgive them after twenty years? You might explain the consequences of family feuds. Explain that sometimes feuds go on for generation after generation with many bloody battles occurring in these "mini-wars". Tell the children how God wants us to settle our differences in a peaceful manner.

Review Sesion

While the children are still gathered around the sandbox scene you could ask some questions to help review the previous lesson.

1. Why did Jacob leave home?
2. What happened his first night out?
3. What promise did God make to Jacob?
4. What did Jacob do with his pillow the next morning?
5. How did Jacob say he would show God that he loved him?

Approach To The Lesson

1. You could draw the children's attention to a map and show them the route which Jacob took when he traveled from Beersheba to Haran. Our lesson opens with Jacob completing his journey and entering the town of his mother's birth.

2. Walk over to the table again using your sandbox scene and call attention to the fact that twenty years have passed as Jacob and Esau meet again. Tell the children that many things happened to Jacob during those twenty years, then lead into your lesson.

The Lesson: Points To Emphasize

1. Jacob loved Rachel and wanted to marry her.

2. Laban tricked Jacob by substituting Leah in the wedding.

3. God has never approved of multiple marriages, although it was a fairly common practice during the history of this period.

4. Jacob was a good husband to both wives. He had a total of twelve sons and one daughter.

5. Jacob became very rich in possessions. He decided to go back home.

6. When Jacob heard that Esau was coming to meet him, he sent men ahead bearing gifts as a peace offering.

7. God changed Jacob's name to Israel. The nation of Israel are descendants of Jacob.

Reinforcing Activities

1. *Praying*. Pray for peace among our families and our nation.

2. *Memory Verse*. Teach the memory verse using the game described in lesson one or any other method you have found effective.

3. *Singing*. Make a picture song book of the song "I Need Thee Every Hour." After teaching the song, discuss how God was with Jacob and how He is with us today.

4. *Role Playing*. Let the children act out the lesson.

5. *Sand Box Scene*. Let the children use the sand box scene to review the lesson. This could be done in place of the role playing or in addition to it.

Application

God wants us to forgive others who have done wrong to us just like Jacob and Esau. Encourage the children to tell of times when they have forgiven someone. Find pictures to represent situations where children need to forgive each other. Discuss these situations in class.

Visual Displays
Bulletin Board

In-Class Worksheet Answers

Page One: Rueben, Simeon, Levi, Judah, Dan, Naphtali, Gad, Asher, Issachar, Zebulun, Joseph, and Benjamin. (Praying, Father, Heaven, forgive.)

Page Two: C, G, B, D, A, E, and F.

1. By working for them. Also he was tricked into marrying Leah.

14

Joseph's Dreams Come True
(Gen. 39-41)
Lesson Aim

1. To teach the children patience in times of stress and to show how God was with Joseph even when he was in the pit and in prison.

2. To teach, through the example of Potophar's wife, that there will always be worldly people who will try to influence us to do evil. If we resist these people and rely on God's word, we will be rewarded.

Preclass Activity

1. Have each child place a star on the attendance chart.

2. Locate pictures that represent times of stress; sickness, fire or accident, unemployment, school or anything else you might think appropriate. As the children sit down, show these pictures to them and ask them if they have ever felt scared during a time when their family suffered through a crisis. Remind them that God sees us through these difficult times and that these times do not last forever.

Review Session

Tell the story from last class, very briefly. Stop and point to one of the students. Let him tell some. Stop and point to another child and let him continue until the last pupil finishes the story.

Approach To The Lesson

1. You could read Matt. 6:31-34. Explain to the children that Joseph was man who did not worry about tomorrow. He took one day at a time and placed his trust and faith in God.

2. You might bring an old tattered coat and a new fine coat to represent a "rags to riches" theme. Hold up the old tattered coat and say the memory verse, "And the Lord was with Joseph, and he was a prosperous man."

The Lesson: Points To Emphasize

1. Joseph was honest and did good work even when sold as a slave.

2. Joseph resisted Potiphar's wife when she tried to convince him to do wrong.

3. Even when in prison and accused wrongly, Joseph still worked hard and was good.

4. God enabled Joseph to interpret the dreams of the cupbearer and baker.

5. God overruled the events in Joseph's life and caused his great promotion because of the faithfulness and love for God.

Reinforcing Activities

1. *Praying.* Word a prayer in which we ask God to give us the faith of Joseph and the assurance that He is with us even in times of distress.

2. *Singing.* Sing "Trust and Obey." Talk of how Joseph trusted and obeyed God. How can we show our trust and obedience to God today?

3. *Memory Verse.* Teach the memory verse using the game mentioned in lesson one or any other method you have found effective. Ask the children to tell you *how* God made Joseph prosperous. Some correct answers to that question being: (1) by being promoted to head over all Egypt and second only to Pharaoh himself or (2) by being lifted from the pit to Potophar's household.

4. *Film Strip or Slides.* If you have access to a film strip or slides and projector, these can be very effective in showing the children how the Egyptians dressed and what Pharaoh's court must have looked like. Any picture that could demonstrate the dress of the times will be very helpful and a good visual aid to the student.

5. *Role Playing.* Allow the children to act out the lesson, making sure that they realize the seriousness of the situation.

6. *Games.* On cards write the words, "Joseph in the pit," "Joseph in Potiphar's house," "Joseph in prison," "Joseph ruler of Egypt." Flash the cards and ask someone in the class to tell you about that specific time in Joseph's life and how God was with him.

Application

Joseph never lost faith in God. On several occasions he was treated very poorly but he always knew that God was with him. In prison, he interpreted the dreams of the cupbearer and baker, giving the glory to God. When, two years later, he interpreted Pharaoh's dream, he acknowledged that God had given him the power.

If we can remember to give God and glory for all good and not question the times when we are in distress, then we can be as faithful as Joseph. You could use the song "Anywhere With Jesus" to teach this application.

Visual Displays
Flannel Graph:
Pharaoh's Court

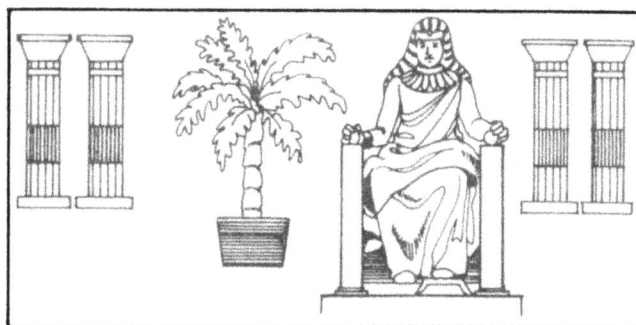

In-Class Worksheet

Answer To Crossword.

ACROSS	DOWN
1. Abraham	2. Adam
3. Eve	3. Eden
4. Animal	5. Issac
6. Esau	7. Ark
9. Jacob	8. Joseph
13. Rainbow	10. Israel
	11. Cain
	12. God

Answer to True-False questions: T, F, T, T, F.

When Israel And His Family Moved To Egypt
(Genesis 42-48)

Lesson Aim

To help the children appreciate God's wisdom and power and His care for those who love and serve Him.

Pre-class Activity

1. Have each child place a final star on their attendance charts. Be sure to let them take the charts home today.

2. On a table you could have some beautiful fruit, bread, fine looking clothes and money. As the children come in, let them examine the items. Tell them that these items represent the riches of the land of Egypt. Ask them if they were really hungry, which of these items would be the most important to them? Discuss what a famine is.

Review Session

You could make a game on a bulletin board by having two columns of people and events. This being the last lesson of this series, you could include in your review items from each lesson. Have a large headed pin with a string tied to it next to each name. Allow the children to come up and match the string with the appropriate phrase in the second column. This can be done by putting another large headed pin next to each phrase. (See Visual Displays.)

Approach To The Lesson

1. You could approach the lesson by using a riddle, "I'm thinking of a man who's brothers threw him into a pit and sold him as a slave. He later became an important man in Egypt and provided food for his brothers. Who is he?"

2. You could ask the children to imagine there is no food in the state of _____ (fill in the state where you are). Friends have brought news that a neighboring state has food. Your parents make plans to go buy food not knowing if they will have to move there or not. Explain to the children that before trucks and trains were invented, people often found themselves in this position. This happened in Bible history to Israel and his family. Then proceed to tell the lesson.

The Lesson: Points To Emphasize

1. Joseph's joy at being re-united with his family.

2. His forgiveness of his brothers.

3. His telling them that God had sent him before them to help save them during the famine.

4. Israel's joy at seeing Joseph again.

5. There were now more than seventy people in the family of Israel. God was already beginning to make a great nation out of Israel.

Reinforcing Activities

1. *Film Strip or Slides*. If you have access to a film strip or slides and projector, these can be a very effective tool in presenting your lesson.

2. *Pictures*. Both Joseph and Israel died in Egypt and were embalmed according to the Egyptian method of mummification. Locate a picture of a mummy to show how they actually looked after the process was completed. Neither Joseph nor Israel believed as the Egyptians that their spirits would return to reuse their bodies here on earth in a second life. It was a very effective method of preserving the bodies. Both Joseph and Israel wanted to be buried in the cave at Machpelah with the other partriarchal fathers.

3. *Map*. Locate the land of Goshen on a map. Show how it was lush and green and provided the best possible place for shepherds.

4. *Singing*. Sing "Trust and Obey." Tell how Joseph and Israel both trusted and obeyed God, and how He took care of them. Tell some ways that God provides for us today.

5. *Praying*. Pray that we will all have the courage of Joseph to trust God completely even during hard times.

6. *Role Playing*. Allow the children to act out the lesson.

Application

God is always with those who love and serve him, even during times of distress. Perhaps the best way to show your children this, is to recall some personal experience from the past and tell the children how God was with you. Little children respond to those who can talk with them and share feelings with them. Encourage them to relate some experience they might have had. Talk about how they might have been afraid at the time. Show them how God has helped them through it all.

Visual Displays

Review game bulletin board.

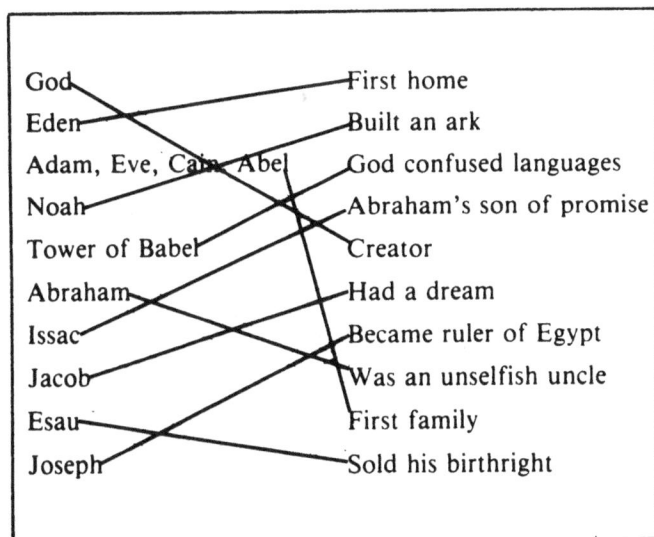

God	First home
Eden	Built an ark
Adam, Eve, Cain, Abel	God confused languages
Noah	Abraham's son of promise
Tower of Babel	Creator
Abraham	Had a dream
Issac	Became ruler of Egypt
Jacob	Was an unselfish uncle
Esau	First family
Joseph	Sold his birthright

The Baby Moses
Ex. 1:8-14, 2:1-10

Lesson Aims

1. Emphasize Moses' mother's faith and trust in God.
2. Encourage the children's faith and trust in God.
3. Encourage the students to be helpful and obedient to their parents.

Pre-class Activity

Bring to class a baby doll, doll clothes, a baby bottle and other items used to care for infants. Let the students "care" for the baby and lead a discussion about how brothers and sisters can help their parents with the younger children in their families. If there is a new baby in your congregation, you could invite the mother and baby as special guests for your pre-class session and discussion.

Review Session

Because this is the first lesson in a new book, you do not have a specific lesson to review; it would be helpful to conduct a brief discussion about how the Israelites came to be in Egypt. Include in your discussion an explanation of how the Egyptians felt about the Israelites and why.

Approach to Lesson

Prepare a bulletin board with pictures of children (cut from magazines, coloring books, or draw your own) helping their parents, working in the yard, feeding pets, etc. Talk about the pictures with the students. Tell them God is pleased when they help and obey their parents. Tell the students that in the lesson they will learn about a girl named Miriam who helped and obeyed her mother and in doing so pleased God as well.

Lesson

Put a baby doll in a basket to show the students as you tell them about the lesson.

Reinforcing Activity

1. Help the children act out the lesson. Props are helpful but not necessary. Some basic props you might use for this lesson are a baby doll, a basket and a crown for the princess. Designate places in the room for the home of Moses' family and the river. The main characters are Miriam, Jochebed, the Egyptian princess and hand-maidens. Other characters you could add, depending on the number of students you wish to include, are Aaron, Moses' father (who can go off to work making bricks and buildings), and additional handmaidens. If you have time, act out the lesson a second time and let the students change roles.

2. Retell the story using flash cards. Make your own flash cards by cutting out pictures and gluing them on index cards or make your own simple drawings. Do not be concerned about your drawing ability. The simplest outlines will get your point across. Your flash cards can be used in a number of ways. Tell the story holding up the cards at the appropriate time, pausing to let the students fill in the word. Hold up a card and ask a question about it; or ask the students to identify the picture and tell how it relates to the lesson.

Application

Prepare a bulletin board on faith. Write each letter in the word Faith on separate sheets of paper or cut out large letters and put across the top of the board. Then cut out and mount the suggested pictures. At the bottom of the board in smaller letters write the words shown with the first letter underlined. Discuss the words and pictures and explain how they relate to the concept of faith.

Fear: Explain that this is not the same kind of fear as we feel for something scary or frightening. This is a fear inspired by respect, the same sort of fear we might feel for our earthly fathers. We do not want to make them angry or unhappy. We want them to be pleased with us.

Ability: We know God has the ability to help us and care for us. We know we can leave things in His hands, just as we know our earthly fathers can guide us and care for us. We have faith in God's ability.

Implicit: Explain that you know this is probably a new word for them. Have them repeat it with you. Use the picture of the sun rising to explain this concept. We know for sure that as long as the world exists the sun will rise every day. There is no question or doubt in our minds about it. We know it implicitly — absolutely, unquestioningly. That is the kind of faith we must try to have, implicit faith.

Trust: We have confidence in God. We know we can rely on our Heavenly Father to care for us.

Hope: Our faith in God gives us hope; we have the hope for happy lives here on earth and more importantly hope of going to heaven to be with God after our lives have ended on earth.

Discuss ways Jochebed's actions in today's lesson illustrate these words.

F	**A**	**I**	**T**	**H**
Fear	Ability	Implicit	Trust	Hope

When Moses Became a Shepherd
Ex. 2:11-25

Lesson Aims

1. Teach the students that it is wrong to hurt people, both in God's eyes and men's eyes.
2. Teach that we should be kind.
3. Show the students that we must carefully guard our anger so that we do not behave in ways that would displease God.

Pre-class Activity

Find pictures illustrating the last lesson or pictures of the land of Egypt and its architecture. Cut each picture into several pieces and put in envelopes. Let the students put the puzzles together and glue them on sheets of construction paper.

Review Session

Use your flash cards from the previous lesson to ask questions and briefly retell the events.

Approach To Lesson

Do some research into the lifestyle of Egyptian royalty and the lifestyle of a shepherd. Find pictures illustrating each in your local library. Discuss the differences with the students and explain that in the lesson for today, they will learn how Moses went from a life of luxury as a prince of Egypt to the lowly life of a shepherd.

Lesson

Tell the lesson emphasizing Moses' compassion for the plight of his people and how his lack of control of his anger resulted in his doing something very wrong. Talk about the cruel and unkind behavior of the shepherds at the well.

Reinforcing Activities

1. Pass out an index card, marked with a large black or red X, to each child. Then retell the lesson making frequent mistakes. Instruct the children to raise their cards in the air each time you make an incorrect statement. Then call on one of the students to identify the error and correct it.

2. On a bulletin board put the headings, "Behavior Pleasing to God? Behavior Displeasing to God?" Write on strips or sheets of paper the following statements:

(1) Moses felt sad because his people were being mistreated.
(2) The Egyptian taskmaster beat the Israelite slave.
(3) Moses killed the Egyptian taskmaster.
(4) The two Israelites argued and fought.
(5) The shepherds drove the sisters away from the well.
(6) Moses helping the girls at the well.
(7) Reuel inviting Moses to his home.

Discuss each situation with the students. Let one of the students pin up a strip under the correct heading.

Application

Go over the words of the song "Angry Words, Oh Let Them Never." You may want to put some of the words on a blackboard or bulletin board. Discuss the subject of anger, including things they get angry about, and how anger should be handled. You might want to ask your songleader to include the song in the worship service.

Moses at the Burning Bush
Ex. 3:1-10; 4:1-9

Lesson Aims

1. Teach that we must do God's will rather than our own.

2. God will be with us and help us do the things which He wants us to do, just as He helped Moses. We can do things with God's help that we could not do by ourselves.

3. God watches over His people and knows their problems.

Pre-class Activity

Help the children make a table-top scene to use to illustrate the lesson. Use heavy white or brown paper such as wrapping paper, poster board or butcher paper cut as wide as the table and long enough for the students to draw a background for the scene (sky, mountains, shrubs). Attach it to the wall immediately above the table. Help the children make pipecleaner figures of Moses and his flock. Make a staff for Moses and attach cotton balls to the pipecleaner sheep. Bring a small branch of leaves and push into a clay base to make it stand up. Let another student glue or tape pieces of red construction paper to the leaves to represent the burning bush.

Review

Who Am I? Read these riddles to your students to review the people and events from the last lesson.

1. I was beaten by an Egyptian taskmaster. Who am I?
2. I saw the Israelite slave being beaten and it made me very angry. Who am I?
3. Moses saw us quarreling. Who are we?
4. Moses was afraid that I would find out that he had killed an Egyptian. Who am I?
5. I am the far-away country Moses traveled to. What is my name?
6. Moses saw us being unkind to seven girls at a well. Who are we?
7. I was the father of the seven girls Moses met at the well. Who am I?

Approach to Lesson

Lead the students in a discussion about times when they had to do things they really did not want to do, perhaps things they were told to do by their teachers or parents. Talk about whether or not they did them and why they did (even though they did not want to). They did them because they know they have to obey their parents and teachers. Then, talk about obeying God and putting God's will before our own. For example, there have probably been activities the children have had to miss in order to attend worship services or times they have told the truth when it seemed easier to tell a lie. Conclude the discussion by telling the children that they are going to learn about a time when God told Moses to do something that Moses really

did not want to do. They will find out whether or not Moses obeyed God.

Lesson

Tell the lesson using the table top scene the students made during the pre-class period.

Reinforcing Activities

1. Take-Aways. Make simple pictures of sheep, the burning bush, a pair of shoes, Egypt (a triangle to represent a pyramid with a palm tree next to it), a rod, a snake, a hand and Aaron (a stick figure of a man). Mount the pictures on a bulletin board in such a way that they can be easily removed and replaced. Have the children close their eyes while you remove one of the pictures. Let one of the students identify the missing picture and explain its significance to the lesson. Replace the picture and repeat the activity, each time removing a different picture.

2. Make a bulletin board divided into two columns labeled "Moses' Excuses, God's Answers." In the first column, list Moses' excuses: (1) He was not important enough to be the leader; (2) The people would not believe God had sent him; (3) He was not a good speaker. In the second column list God's answer to each of Moses' excuses: (1) Moses would be representing God, not himself; (2) God would give Moses the power to perform certain miraculous signs; (3) God would provide a helper, Aaron, to speak for Moses. Discuss the excuses and God's answers. Try covering or removing God's answers, then read the excuses one at a time, letting the children explain God's answers to each one.

Application

Find pictures of children attending worship services, praying, studying, working around their homes, visiting the sick or elderly, etc. Explain to the students that just as God had a job for Moses to do, He has things for us to do in service to Him. Show the pictures and discuss them with your students. Explain that these are some of the duties God has given us.

Moses and Aaron Before Pharaoh
Ex. 5; 7:8-13

1. Teach that God watches over His people and knows their troubles and sorrows.
2. Emphasize that God has all power and authority, even over rulers of countries and heads of government.

Pre-class Activity

Print sentences containing events and facts from the three previous lessons on a blackboard, bulletin board, or poster board, omitting some of the words. Print the omitted words on pieces of paper cut to fit the blanks and place them in a box. Let the students look through the box to find the missing words and use tape or thumb tacks to place the missing words in the correct blanks.

Review

Use "Jeopardy". This activity is conducted much like the television game show. Put up the four headings and underneath each one put five large index cards. Number one side of each card. On the other side of each index card write a question. Let the students take turns selecting a category and a number. Read the question aloud. If the student answers the question correctly, give him the card. If he is incorrect, put the card back in its place (another student may choose it). Categories and questions:

Moses At The Burning Bush
1. What was Moses doing when he saw the burning bush?
2. Whose voice came from the burning bush?
3. What was Moses told to remove?
4. What was so unusual about this bush?
5. What did God say about the ground Moses was standing on?

God's Job For Moses
1. What was the special job God had for Moses?
2. Who did God tell Moses to talk to?
3. Where did God tell Moses to go?
4. What did God tell Moses to say to Pharaoh?
5. Was Moses happy about this special job God had given him?

Moses' Excuses
1. Moses said, "I can't do that. I'm only a shepherd. No one will listen to me. I'm not _____ enough."
2. Who did God tell Moses to take with him to speak for him?
3. Moses said, "The people won't _____ me."
4. Moses said, "I can't _____ well enough."
5. What was God's answer to Moses when he said the people would not believe him?

God's Special Signs
1. What special sign did Moses first see?
2. What happened to Moses' rod?
3. What happened to Moses' hand?
4. What did God tell Moses would happen to the water?
5. What was the purpose of these special signs?

Approach to Lesson

Make a crown from yellow construction paper or cardboard covered with gold. Show it to the students and use it to introduce a discusssion about kings and queens and heads of state and their authority. Include in the discussion the fact that government leaders have authority over all their citizens, but God has all authority even over the heads of government.

Lesson

Tell the lesson emphasizing Pharaoh's refusal to obey God, the elders acceptance of Moses as their leader, and the worsening of the conditions under which the Israelites were living and working.

Reinforcing Activities

1. Read and Do. Print questions and instruction based on facts from the lesson on slips of paper. Put the strips of paper in a box, jar, or bag and let the children take turns drawing the strips of paper and following the instructions or answering the question. Here are some examples:

1. Who went with Moses to see Pharaoh?
2. Name the sign Moses performed before Pharaoh.
3. Name something the Israelites used to make bricks.

2. Read the lesson from the student's book, pausing frequently to let the students fill in the proper word. For example, read, "Moses was on his way back to *(pause)* when he met his brother, *(pause)*."

Application

Conduct a discussion on authority. Cut out and label these silhouettes and let the children take turns lining them up in their proper order of authority. You could also mention other figures in authority such as teachers, policemen, elders, etc. Be sure to stress that obedience to any earthly authority is always conditioned upon its agreement with God's will.

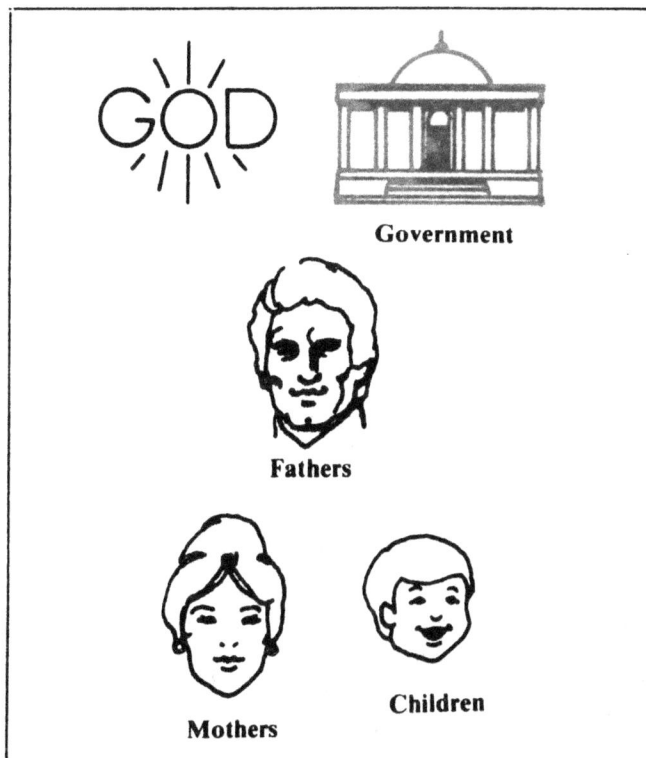

GOD

Government

Fathers

Mothers

Children

The Plagues That Came Upon Egypt
Ex. 7:20-25; 10:2; 11:3

Lesson Aims

1. Teach that God controls the universe and has power over nature and the elements as well as all living things.
2. Teach that God punishes those who disobey Him.
3. Teach the importance of obedience to God.

Pre-class Activity

Write the scripture references of the memory verses for the last four lessons on a blackboard or piece of poster board. Give each child strips of construction paper and have them copy one or more of the verses on the strips to make bookmarkers. After they have copied a memory verse, help them look up the scripture and place the bookmarker in the proper place.

Review

Find pictures illustrating events from the past lessons (look in past class handouts, class books, or draw your own simple stick figure pictures). Include some pictures illustrating things your class has not studied. Let the students put the pictures in the proper order, pulling out the pictures that do not fit in the sequence. (Save these pictures for the pre-class activity in your next lesson.)

Approach to Lesson

Bring to class pictures of, or books about insects — or even better, bring in real insects, a frog, a fly, a grasshopper (to represent the locusts). Discuss with the students how they feel about bugs or insects. Then ask how they would feel about finding frogs in their oven or even in their beds. Help your students realize how repulsive and troublesome these plagues must have been. Explain to the students that in the lesson for today they will learn about these and other terrible things that happened in the land of Egypt as a result of Pharaoh and his people refusing to obey God.

Lesson

Tell the lesson emphasizing Pharaoh's disobedience and the results, stressing the fact that God protected His own people even while the plagues were falling on Egypt. Use the pictures or insects you brought in to illustrate some of the plagues.

Reinforcing Activities

1. Take-Aways. Find pictures representing each plague and mount on construction paper circles. Mount them on a bulletin board in such a way they can be easily removed and replaced. Go over each picture to be sure the students understand what they represent. Have the students turn their backs or close their eyes while you remove one of the pictures. Then have the students look and try to identify the missing plague. If you repeat this activity several times, the students should be able to name all the plagues.

2. Pass out a card to each child with the word "wrong" printed on it. Tell the lesson again, making frequent errors. Instruct the students to raise their cards in the air when they hear an error. Then call on one of the students to identify the error.

Application

Discuss the importance of obedience to God. On a blackboard put the two headings "Obedience" and "Disobedience." Ask for suggestions from the students for a list of things we do in obedience to God. Then list the things that would constitute disobedience to God. For example, we attend worship services in obedience to God. We are being disboedient when we fail to come together to worship God. Talk briefly about the results of disobedience both in this life and after this life.

How the Israelites Left Egypt
Ex. 12:29-36; 13:17-22

Lesson Aims

1. Teach that God cares for and protects His children.
2. Show that just as God gave the Israelites specific rules to follow, God has given us specific commands that must be obeyed.
3. Show that those who obey God will be saved, those who disobey God will be punished.

Pre-class Activity

Use the series of pictures from the review activity in Lesson 5. Write incorrect captions on each picture. Let the students examine each picture caption and correct them on their own individual sheets of paper. Check your students' work.

Review

Draw this crossword puzzle on the blackboard. You do not need to put up the clues, just read them aloud. Call on a child to select a clue number, read it and let the child fill in the answer. Take turns until the pizzle is completed.

Approach to Lesson

Bring to class a piece of regular white bread and a piece of the unleavened bread such as is used in the Lord's Supper. Bring a cookbook with a basic bread recipe and a packet of yeast. Discuss the differences in the two types of bread. Explain that although the ingredients are very much the same, there is one important difference. Explain the process of leavening and be sure to point out (using your recipe) that the rising process takes quite a while and when the Israelites finally left Egypt, they did not have time to wait for their bread to rise. Tell the students that in the lesson for today, they would learn why the Israelites were in such a hurry to leave Egypt.

Lesson

Tell the lesson emphasizing the regulations which God told the Israelites to observe, Pharaoh finally permitting the Israelites to leave Egypt, the fact that the Israelites were spared, and their hasty departure from the land of Egypt.

Reinforcing Activities

1. Divide the children into groups of two or three. To each "team" give a list of 3 or 4 words — people, places, events — connected with the lesson. Give the teams a few minutes to make up a question about each word on their list. Go around to each team and check their questions and answers.

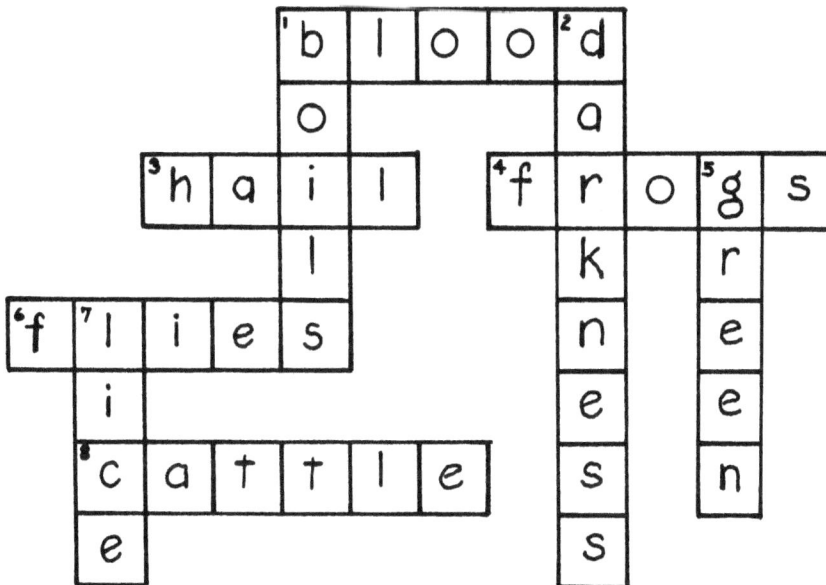

Clues

Across
1. The waters of Egypt turned to *blood.*
3. Frozen rain. (hail)
4. What came out when Aaron stretched his hand over the waters? (frogs)
6. There came a "grievous swarm" of these. (flies)
8. These animals became very sick and died. (cattle)

Down
1. Sores that covered men and animals. (boils)
2. This covered the land and the people could not see. (darkness)
5. Ex. 10:15 tells us there remained not any *(green)* thing after the locusts came.
7. All of the dust of the land became *(lice).*

25

2. After you have checked the questions and answers, let the members of each team read a question out loud to the class. Let the student who reads the question call on one of the students (not on his team) to answer the question. Continue the activity until all the questions have been read aloud.

Application

Prepare a bulletin board titled "Signs to Show We Are God's People." Explain that just as the blood on the doorposts identified God's people on the night of the passover, certain things we do should identify us today as God's people. Draw a door with the doorposts and blood to put in the center of your bulletin board. Around the door put pictures, words and scripture references telling ways we show we are God's people. For example: clothes — our modest apparel shows that we are God's people. Love (Jn. 13:35) — by this shall all men know that ye are my disciples, if ye have love one to another. Worship — we worship God by attending worship services, singing and praying. Obedience — we are obedient to parents, teachers, the government. Purity — we guard against evil and evil appearances.

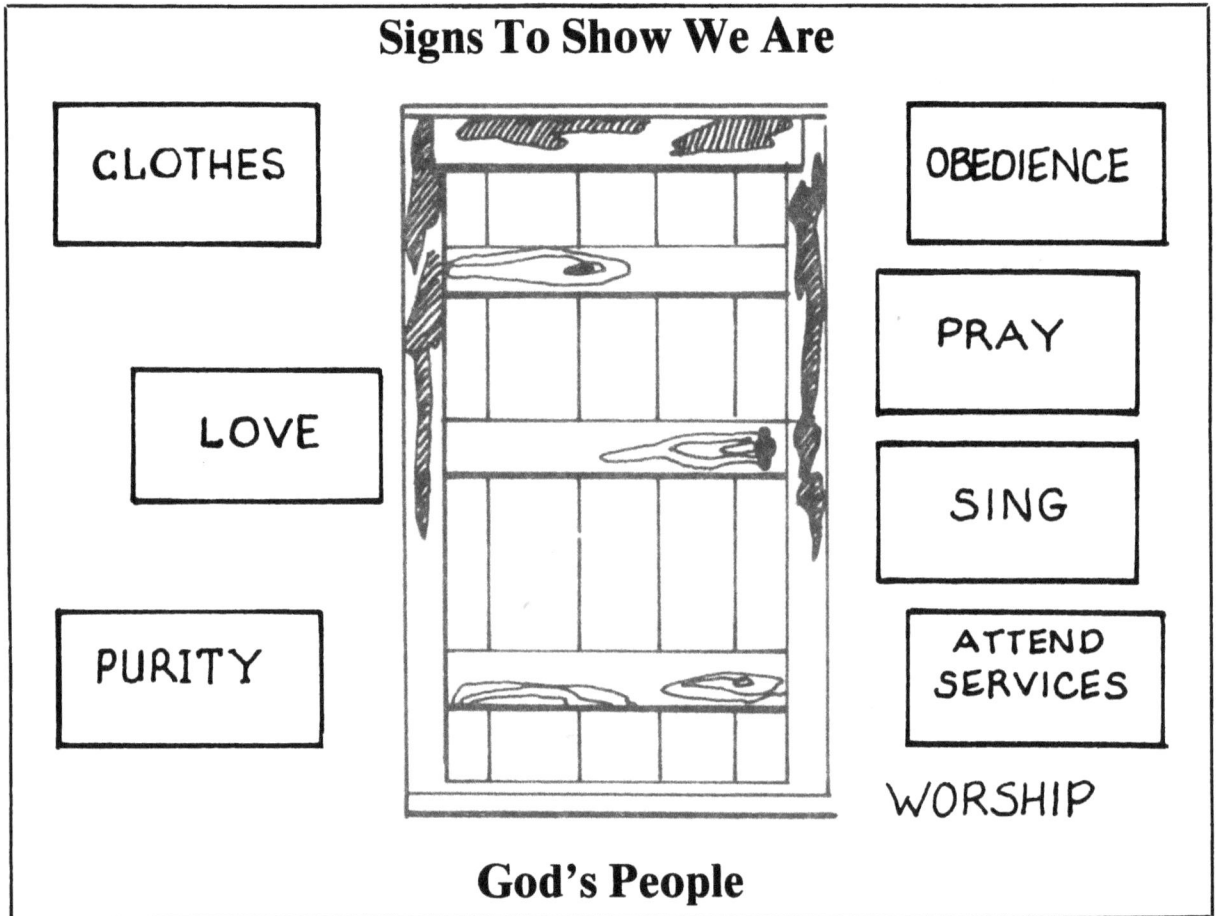

Signs To Show We Are

CLOTHES

OBEDIENCE

LOVE

PRAY

SING

PURITY

ATTEND SERVICES

WORSHIP

God's People

How the People Walked Through the Sea
Ex. 13:20-22; 14

Lesson Aims

1. Show that God leads us today by His word just as surely as He led the Israelites.
2. God will help us overcome obstacles when we follow Him.

Pre-class Activity

Help your students make a songbook illustrating the words to the hymn "He Leadeth Me." Cut pictures out of magazines to illustrate each line of the song (the chorus and 1 or 2 of the verses). Let the children glue the pictures on sheets of construction paper and print the words to the line they illustrate. Put the book together with tape, staples or brads. You will use this book in the application portion of your lesson.

Review

Make up questions based on the events of the last lesson with one word answers. Print the answers on index cards and tape them on the wall. Read the questions and let the students take turns selecting the answers from the words on the wall.

Approach to Lesson

Bring to class a large pan or baking dish filled with water, a toy boat, a toy airplane and also pictures of different types of boats if you can find them. Show the pictures of the boats and talk about traveling over water. Ask one of the students to try to divide the water in the dish into two parts and talk about why it cannot be done. Explain that, in the lesson for today, they will learn about a time when the Israelites were in terrible trouble and were faced with that very problem and how God helped them.

Lesson

Tell the lesson emphasizing God's method of leading the Israelites by night and day, Pharaoh's army in pursuit, the miracle of the crossing of the sea, the destruction of the wicked and the salvation of God's people.

Reinforcing Activities

1. Write the major events of the lesson on strips of paper. Pass out a strip to each student and then have the students read the strips and put themselves in the proper order. Then read all the strips in the correct sequence. If your class is small, you may have to do this two or three times to tell the whole lesson. If your class is large, do the activity once, then have the students change strips and do it again.

2. Read these riddle/rhymes to the students and let them fill in the last word. (Save these riddle/rhymes for your review in the next lesson.)

1. Nine terrible plagues on Egypt came, but Pharaoh's mind remained the *same*.
2. The tenth plague came and as you know Pharaoh finally let God's people *go*.
3. A pillar of fire gave them light and helped to guide them in the *night*.
4. A cloud by day would help them know the way God wanted them to *go*.
5. They walked until they came to be standing at the edge of a great *sea*.
6. They turned and saw coming from behind Egyptians! Pharaoh had changed his *mind*.
7. First God caused the cloud to come between so the Israelites could not be *seen*.
8. We were better off in Egypt, they began to cry, than coming here where we might *die*.
9. First Moses prayed, then obeyed God, he raised his arm and waved his *rod*.
10. A strong wind blew and on either hand a wall of water was caused to *stand*.
11. On each side the walls stood high; where Israel walked the land was *dry*.
12. When God's people had crossed safe and well, Moses waved his rod, the waters *fell*.
13. Egypt disobeyed, at what a cost! The waters fell; their lives were *lost*.
14. When we, like Israel, His will obey, God guides and cares for us *Today*.

Application

Teach the words of the song "He Leadeth Me" using the illustrated songbook your students made in the pre-class period. Discuss how God leads us today.

per order and then read the verse aloud. You can have the students exchange strips and repeat the activity a couple of times. Discuss the meaning of the verse phrase by phrase.

How the People Were Fed in the Wilderness
Ex. 16:1-18

Lesson Aims

1. Teach that God knows the needs of His people.
2. Show that God answers those needs.
3. Show that, in order to take advantage of God's blessings, we must obey His will.

Pre-class Activity

Help your students make an illustrated book titled "Thank You, God, for the Food We Eat." Bring magazine pictures of different types of foods, animals such as cows and chickens, farmers and farms, fields of grain, mothers or chefs cooking — any pictures showing food, its preparation and production, etc. Bring construction paper, glue, crayons and what you will need to put your book together. Help the students glue pictures onto the construction paper sheets and think of captions for the pictures such as, "Thank you, God, for the farmers who grow our food." "Thank you, God, for cows who give us milk and butter." You can use this book in the approach to the lesson.

Review

Read the riddle/rhymes from the previous lesson for your review activity.

Approach to Lesson

Read through the book your students made in the pre-class period. Discuss the ways God provides us with food. Explain that in the lesson, they will learn how the Israelites were fed by God while they were journeying in the wilderness.

Lesson

Tell the lesson emphasizing the Israelites repeated grumblings, God's way of providing them with water, God's sending the manna and quails, and how God gave the Israelites special instructions about how to go about gathering the food He had given them.

Reinforcing Activities

1. Read the lesson from the student's book. Pause frequently to let the students fill in the words for you.
2. Make up a number of questions from the lesson with single word answers. Print the answers on cards or strips of paper and pass them out, two or three cards to each student. Then read the questions aloud and have the students with the correct answers hold up their cards.

Application

Write the memory verse on cut-up strips of paper with two or three words on each strip. Hand out one strip to each student and help them arrange themselves in the pro-

How God Gave The Law
Ex. 19:16 - 20:17

Lesson Aims

1. Teach that God gave the Israelites rules to obey.
2. God has given us rules to live by, too.
3. Many of the rules God gave the Israelites are very similiar to those that are applicable today.

Pre-class Activity

Let your students help you make an "Obeying the Law" bulletin board. Before your students arrive put the words "Obeying the Law" in the middle of the bulletin board. Above the words, put a picture of a Bible and beneath the picture, the words "God's Law." Cut appropriately colored construction paper into the shape of road signs (red for *stop,* yellow for *yield,* white for *speed limits* signs, etc.). Make a traffic light outline and let the students glue on the red, yellow and green circles for the lights. Using stencils or pre-cut letters, help the students put the letters on the signs. Then let them mount their signs around the words on the bulletin board. You can use this bulletin board in both the approach to the lesson and the application of the lesson.

Review

On a blackboard write the words "Eating with the Israelites." Below the title, write the words *"Who, What, When, How, Why."* Then go over each word asking these questions. *Who* gave the Israelites their food? *What* did God give the Israelites to eat? *When* did the quails come? *When* did the Israelites gather the manna? *How* did they get the quails? *How* did they get the manna? *Why* did God feed the Israelites? After you have gone over the words and the answers you may want to ask more specific questions on other points from the lesson not covered by the words.

Approach to Lesson

Using your "Obeying the Law" bulletin board, discuss in general terms the traffic signs and what they mean. Ask what would happen without these signs. Talk about the purpose of traffic signs — they keep us from hurting ourselves and each other.

Lesson

Tell the lesson emphasizing the way Moses received the law, the commandments, the meaning of the sabbath and that it is the only one of the commandments that is not similar to those given to us as Christians.

Application

Using your bulletin board again, point out that the purpose of all laws, including traffic laws, is to help people live peacefully and happily together. Emphasize this fact by asking the students what would happen if there were no laws against stealing or hitting people, etc. Talk about God's laws for us today, where the Christians can find them? Tell that, in addition to helping us all live together happily, we obey the Bible in order to please God. Now go over the traffic signs again using them to remind us of some of God's laws, for example: *Stop* doing things that are wrong, *Yield* not to temptation, *RR Crossing* might remind us to watch out for things coming our way that might cause us to disobey God such as the wrong companions, anger, etc.

Reinforcing Activities

1. Put up a chart listing the Ten Commandments (you may wish to paraphrase some of them). Help the students read the chart out loud.
2. Go over each commandment, discussing its meaning. Have the students turn away from the chart and try to name as many of the commandments as they can.

The Golden Calf
Ex. 32

Lesson Aims

1. Teach that idolatry is wrong (and is still practiced by some people today).

2. Show that God is greater than any of His creations and only the Creator is to be worshipped.

3. Show that displeasing God will result in unhappiness for us.

Pre-class Activity

Bring modeling clay to class. Let the students mold an animal, then roll it up and begin again. This activity will be discussed during the approach to the lesson.

Review

See how many of the commandments your students can name. Write them on a blackboard (in simple form) as your students name them. Help them look up any which they could not remember. Discuss briefly what each meant.

Approach

Hold a piece of modeling clay in your hand and shape it into a simple animal form as you talk. Tell the students about the pre-class activity. Then ask the students who participated in the pre-class activity some questions like these: What sort of things did we make? What did we do with them when we were finished? Do you think those little figures could have helped us do anything? Why not?

Discuss with all the students the fact that in many parts of the world people worship and trust in figures made of clay or wood or stone. They worship figures they have made with their own hands and could as easily destroy. Explain that the Egyptians had worshipped idols. Show the students pictures of idols from books on ancient Egypt, Greece, and Rome. Talk with them about the futility of worshipping an animal or a piece of wood or stone. Lead into the lesson by saying that they are going to learn about a time the Israelites turned away from the living God and began to worship one of these statues.

Lesson

Tell the lesson emphasizing where Moses was and what he was doing, that the people requested an idol, that Aaron was approving the people's request, God's anger at what the people were doing, and Moses' anger at what the people were doing.

Reinforcing Activities

1. Write the main points of the lesson on strips of paper. Give one strip to each student and let him read his strips aloud. Then help them arrange themselves in the proper order. Then read the strips again telling the major events of the lesson in their proper order.

2. Take-aways. Make simple pictures of a mountain (to represent where Moses was), an idol, golden jewelry, a calf, a man (to represent Aaron), an angry face (to illustrate how Moses felt), broken tablets, and a bowl or container of dirty-looking water. Mount the pictures on a bulletin board in such a way that they can be easily removed and replaced. Have the children close their eyes while you remove one of the pictures. Let one of the students identify the missing picture and explain its significance to the lesson. Replace the picture and repeat the activity, each time removing a different picture.

Application

Lead your students in a discussion about religious medals, pictures, statues, and figurines. A book on Roman and Greek Orthodox Catholicism would be a good source of pictures. Many religious bookstores gives away pamphlets with pictures of religious medals, etc., that you can show to your students to illustrate what you are talking about.

The Tabernacle
Ex. 35:4-29; 36:2-7

Lesson Aims

1. Teach the students about the structure of the tabernacle.

2. Show the difference in the way the Israelites worshipped and the way we worship today.

3. Emphasize that the physical building today is of no importance. The Church is made up of people, not bricks or stones.

Pre-class Activity

For several of your activities today, you are going to use a simple floorplan of the tabernacle marked on the floor with masking tape. Before any of your students arrive, mark the corners with masking tape x's. Let the students put down the tape to complete the outline of the floorplan., Then help them place X's over the spots where the furnishings stood. Make your floorplan large enough for the students to walk around in it. Here is a simple diagram of the tabernacle and its furnishings.

A. The Courtyard
B. Altar of burnt offering
C. Laver
D. Holy Place
E. Table of shewbread
F. The candlestick
G. The altar
H. Most Holy Place
I. Ark of the Covenant
J. Veil

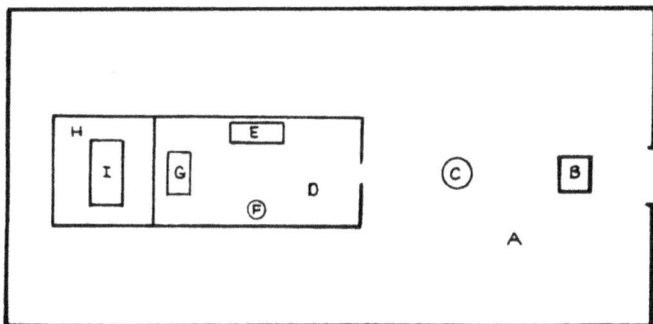

Review Session

Who Said It? Read these statements and let the children identify who might have made the statement.

1. I was on a mountain talking with God.
2. We asked Aaron to be our leader and make an idol for us to worship.
3. I went along with what the people wanted to do, even though it was wrong.
4. We brought our golden jewelry to Aaron.
5. I fashioned a calf out of the gold.
6. We danced around the calf and worshipped it.
7. I was so angry with the Israelites that I threw down the stones with the Ten Commandments on them.

8. I told Moses that the people made me do those wrong things.
9. I threw the powder from the ground-up calf into water.
10. We had to drink the nasty water.

Approach to Lesson

Make a bulletin board with pictures of church buildings. (This will also be used in the application portion of the lesson.) Talk about the buildings and explain that the Israelites worshipped in a very different sort of place. Explain that the diagram on the floor will help them see how the tabernacle was set up and furnished. Explain that their place of worship was a tent and that it could be put up and taken down as they moved from place to place.

Lesson

Find some reference books and read about the tabernacle and its furnishings. Find books with pictures of the tabernacle's furnishings to show the students. Using your floorplan, explain it and show where the furnishings were and the purpose of each. Include in your explanation the contents of the Ark of the Covenenat.

Reinforcing Activities

1. Conduct a "guided tour" of the tabernacle. Ask the students questions as you make the tour. What would be here? What was it for? What would we see in this room? What was this part of the tabernacle called? etc.

2. Find the Spot. Line the students up and then give individual students instructions to go stand in a certain place. For example, go to the Most Holy Place. Go stand where the laver was. Go to where the altar stood, and so on.

Application

Using your bulletin board, talk about the fact that where we worship today is not important. The Church could meet under a tree or in someone's home or in a school building. The Church is composed of Christians.

Aaron and His Sons
Ex. 29; Lev. 10:1-3

Lesson Aims

1. Explain the office of the priest and the purpose of the priesthood.
2. Teach that all Christians are priests and the Christ is our high priest.
3. Show through the story of Nadab and Abihu that disobedience to God will be punished.

Pre-class Activity

Do some research on the garments of the High Priest. Draw simple illustrations of the various things they wore and cut them out. Help the students paste them on an outline figure of a man. If several students are usually present during this period, make more than one set of garments and men so all the students present can dress one of them.

Review Session

On a blackboard draw the diagram of the floor plan of the tabernacle. Let the students mark the spots where the various rooms and furnishings were and explain the purpose of each.

Approach to Lesson

Find pictures illustrating the ways we worship God: singing, praying, taking the Lord's Supper, etc. Talk about the practice and purpose of each. Discuss the fact that the Israelites worshipped God in some different ways than we do today such as offering burnt sacrifices and purification processes. They also had men called priests doing special jobs to help them in their worship. Tell the students that they are going to learn about the priests today and two in particular who disobeyed God and how they were punished.

Lesson

Find pictures illustrating the garments of the high priest. Explain the different parts of his clothing and their purpose or symbolism. Point out that only Aaron and his sons could be priests. Explain that the priests were go-betweens for the Israelites and God, offering prayers, incense, and sacrifices. Describe the major duties of the priests and the high priest. Tell about Nadab and Abihu's disobedience and its results.

Reinforcing Activities

1. Draw this crossword puzzle on a sheet of posterboard and read the clues aloud, letting the students come up and fill in the words.

Across

3. The short tunic worn by the high priest.

Down

1. Only the high priest could enter the Most Holy _____.

5. Only he and his sons could serve as priests.
7. He disobeyed God and was punished.
8. Only Aaron and his _____ could be priests.
9. What the high priest had around the hem of his garment.

2. The twelve stones the high priest wore represented the twelve _____.
4. Aaron and his sons were _____.
6. One of Aaron's sons who disobeyed God.

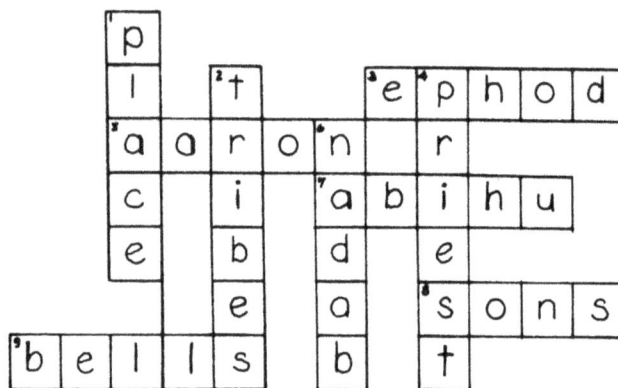

2. Pass out index cards to each student, one marked "T" and one marked "F." Read these statements and have the students hold up the appropriate cards. Let them correct the incorrect statements.

1. Aaron and his sons were given a special job.
2. The priests never disobeyed God.
3. The high priest wore a special necklace called an ephod.
4. The 12 stones the high priest wore represented the twelve commandments.
5. Nadab was Aaron's father.
6. Nadab and Abihu were brothers.
7. Nadab and Abihu were shepherds.
8. The high priest was the only person who could enter the Most Holy Place.
9. God was angry with Nadab and Abihu because they said the wrong prayer.
10. Nadab and Abihu were destroyed with fire.
11. Christ is our high priest today.

Application

Scramble the words of the memory verse and write them on the blackboard. Let the students draw lines to connect the words in their proper order. Explain the meaning of the memory verse as it relates to the lesson.

Moses Leads God's People
Review

Lesson Aims

1. Review the major characters and events covered in this series of lessons.

2. Review the applications to their own lives made in each lesson.

Pre-class Activity

On colored sheets of construction paper, have the students write the memory verse from each lesson. Put the sheets together with the complete set of memory verses.

Review

Read each of the memory verses. Let the students identify the lesson the memory verse is from (what they studied in connection with the verse).

Who's who?

Write these names on index cards and tape them on a wall. Read the clues and let the students select the proper names to identify all the characters they have studied in this series of lessons.

Moses: the leader of the Israelites.

Aaron: the brother of Moses.

Miriam: the sister of Moses.

Princess: found Moses at the river's edge.

Jochebed: the mother of Moses.

Pharaoh: the king of the Egyptians.

Reuel: the father-in-law of Moses.

Nadab: a priest who disobeyed God.

Abihu: another priest who disobeyed God.

The Ten Commandments

Write the Ten Commandments on a blackboard with some important words from each omitted. Read the commandments and let the students fill in the missing words.

The Tabernacle

Mount a diagram of the floorplan of the tabernacle on a bulletin board. On small squares of paper write words identifying the furnishings and rooms of the tabernacle. Let the students put them in the appropriate places on the diagram with thumb tacks.

Jeopardy

See lesson 4, Review, for the instructions for preparing this activity. Make up questions to cover the major events from all the lessons. Here are some suggested headings that should help you cover all the major events.

1. Moses In Egypt (covering birth and early manhood).
2. When Moses Left Egypt (covering why he left, where he went, and what happened to him there).
3. God Speaks to Moses (covering the events at the burning bush, the reunion of Moses and Aaron, and their first appearances before Pharaoh).
4. The Plagues (covering the nine plagues, the passover, and the Israelites leaving Egypt).
5. God Cares for His People (covering the crossing of the sea and being fed in the wilderness).
6. God's Law and Israel's Disobedience (covering the events surrounding the giving of the ten commandments and the worship of the golden calf; you have already covered the actual commandments).

Traveling With The Tribes Of Israel
Ex. 32:1-10, Num. 10:11-28, 11:1-23

Lesson Aims

1. Instill a deep faith and trust in God as supreme planner and protector for their lives.

2. Teach the student God's plan for building the tabernacle and introduce the idea that the Old Testament contains shadows of New Testament realities. This can be done by comparing the tabernacle with the church.

3. Teach God's care and providence in guiding the children of Israel by the pillar of cloud and fire, in feeding them with manna, and by providing clothing that did not rot.

4. Introduce the children to some basic geographical areas of the Bible lands.

Preclass Activity

1. As the children enter the room, direct their attention to an activity table upon which you have a cardboard model of the tabernacle. Point to the different rooms and the items of furniture located in each room. You might make a statement like this: "Here is the candlestick which gave light to the Holy Place." Follow it with a question such as, "What do you suppose gives light to the church today?" Explain to the children that the church is *not* the building; instead, we worship God in our hearts and God's word, the Bible, gives light to our hearts. Make a game out of this by associating the various items of the physical tabernacle with their spiritual equivalent in the New Testament. Even though the children may not fully understand the deepest meaning, they can associate the two and begin to see how we live under a spiritual law as compared to a physical law. These truths will need to be taught many times as the children grow. Make their first introduction to it interesting and exciting.

2. Make a large, simple map showing the Mediterranean Sea, the promised land, Sea of Galilee, etc. You might use the attendance chart as a model. Make overlays of construction paper to make a puzzle with which the children can work. You might use a small bulletin board and make a game out of placing the bodies of water, promised land, Jordan River, etc. in the proper place on the map. Each class period allow the children some time to work with the puzzle map. With each period, add the area or city appropriate for the lesson of that day. By the end of this series of lessons, the places will be very familiar and the students should be able to fill in a simple map. See in-class worksheet for lesson thirteen.

3. Write vocabulary words on the board and discuss.

Review Session

1. Discuss how the children of Israel had left Egypt. They were no longer slaves, but are a nation of people who are very special in God's plan for man.

2. Discuss and plan a class outing to be held on a Saturday sometime during this series. A suggestion would be to have a simulated wilderness wandering in a local park. Have the children follow the teacher (who would represent Moses) while walking around the park you could use any natural features to help the children see what it could have been like.

A. *Campgrounds.* Stopping at this point, you could discuss the nomadic life they led for forty years.

B. *Stream.* Here you could discuss how they crossed the Jordan River into the promised land. If a foot bridge is available, you might mention how you are crossing with the aid of a bridge, but God caused the waters to divide so His people could enter on dry land.

C. *Nature Trail.* You might discuss, as you walk along, how the children of Israel did not have a path to follow but they were led by the cloud.

D. *Birds.* You could discuss the quail that the people begged for and how God sent it to them.

E. *Picnic Grounds.* While eating lunch you might discuss how you had to bring your lunch today, but God provided manna for His people every day.

Approach To The Lesson

1. Give each student their attendance chart. Show the area where the children of Israel crossed the Red Sea. Have them put a big red "one" on that location as this is the place where the wilderness wanderings began. Now have them place a brown triangle cut from construction paper on the location of Mt. Sinai. Be sure you do the same thing with your large puzzle map. Tell them how special this mountain is because this is where the children of Israel become the nation of Israel with God speaking to Moses, His chosen leader.

2. You could hold up a pair of worn shoes. You might say, "These shoes are only one-year old and look how worn they are. Today we are going to talk about some special shoes, those worn by the nation of Israel which lasted for forty years, because God did not let them wear out. This was only one of the ways He took care of His people."

The Lesson-Points To Emphasize

1. The events that had taken place at Sinai:
   A. Giving of the law of Moses.
   B. People making the golden calf.
   C. We do not live by the old law today because God gave us a new law when Jesus Christ came and died.

2. God was directing the people and taking care of them by:
   A. A pillar of fire and cloud to lead them.
   B. Manna for food.
   C. Clothing not wearing out.

3. The tabernacle was a tent-like structure. Emphasize the people's generosity in giving precious cloth and jewels so that it could be completed.

Reinforcing Activities

1. *Film Strip.* If you have access to a film strip or slide projector, this can be a very valuable reinforcement to your lesson. The *Visualized Bible Study Series* by Jule Miller (lesson two, the Mosaical Age) is excellent for this lesson. By using the slides from Sinai to the building of the tabernacle, you can cover the lesson in about twenty minutes time. There is an accompanying cassette tape which could also be used. This would still leave time for other activities.

2. *Praying.* Always include at least one prayer in each class session. In wording the prayer you might ask God to give each of us the faith that Moses had to always obey all of God's commandments.

3. *Singing.* Sing "Savior Like a Shepherd Lead Us." See the in-class worksheet to be used with this activity. Explain the words of the song. Compare the children of Israel being led by God to a shepherd leading his sheep.

4. *Puzzle Map.* Take down the overlays from your puzzle map. Let each student, one at a time, place the geographical pieces in the proper place on the puzzle map.

5. *Memory Verse.* Teach the memory verse. One way is to make a game of it. Write each word of the entire memory verse on a separate three-by-five card. Pass the cards out and have the children place them in the proper order. If a bulletin board is available, allow the children to come up one at a time and tack their card in the appropriate place.

Application

God provided everything His people ever needed. When they were good and trusted in Him, they were blessed; but when they were bad, they were punished. God has promised us today that He will provide for us. We are promised food and clothing. We have a promised land to go to when we die, but like the children of Israel, we must obey God's commandments to receive the rewards.

Visual Displays

For your bulletin board:

Tabernacle

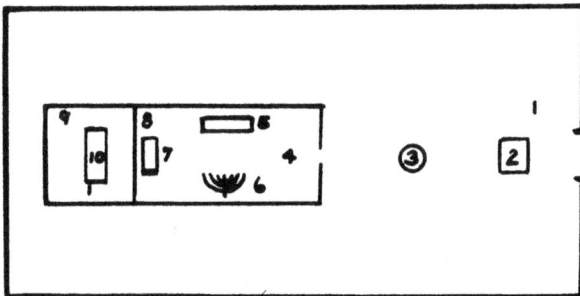

O.T.

1. Courtyard
2. Altar of burnt offering
3. Laver
4. Holy Place
5. Table of Shewbread
6. Candlestick
7. Altar of incense
8. Veil

9. Most Holy Place
10. Ark of covenant: Animal blood

N.T.

1. World
2. Sacrifice of Christ
3. Christian Baptism
4. Church
5. Lord's Supper
6. God's word
7. Prayers
8. Christians from heathens
9. Heaven
10. Christ's blood

In-Class Worksheets

After teaching the song, have the children cross out the incorrect words on the appropriate worksheet. Compare how a shepherd leads his sheep with how a rancher drives his cattle. Help the children see that God was leading His children. No one is ever *forced* to follow God. Stress the blessings and rewards of being a child of God and obeying Him. The worksheets can be used as a review of today's lesson. Stress that Mt. Sinai was the beginning of God's laws being written down for His people to follow. Also touch on the new law that Jesus established when he died on the cross. Help the children see that we, too, have a promised land to look forward to.

The Twelve Spies
Num. 13; 14:26-38

Lesson Aims:

1. Show how the Israelites could have entered the promised land if they had had faith in God.

2. Stress their punishment for lack of faith.

3. Instill a deep faith in God to know He causes events to happen to accomplish His purpose even though these events do not make sense to us.

Preclass Activity:

1. Point out on your puzzle map the point where the Israelites are in this lesson. Have the children place a marker on their attendance charts signifying the geographical feature they will be studying. Some of the early arrivals might enjoy working the puzzle map and quizzing each other as to what events have happened where.

2. After all the children have arrived, ask one of the boys to lead a prayer. This will set the mood for your class and encourage the young men to take a lead as they will someday be required to do.

3. Go over vocabulary words and tie them into the lesson.

Review Session:

1. Write the following questions on 3" x 5" cards and tape them under the chairs. Ask the students to reach underneath their chair and get their question. Each one must then answer their question. Here are some questions to use:

   A. What was the tabernacle?

   B. How did the people know when God wanted them to move?

   C. What did Moses do when he saw the people worshipping the golden calf?

   D. What was the name of the mountain where God gave the law to Moses?

   E. How were the people fed?

   F. Where is our promised land today?

Approach To The Lesson

1. Hold up some grapes, figs, and pomegranates. Pass them around the room. (Real fruit are best, but artificial will do.) You could explain that these are some of the fruits which the spies brought back with them from their mission. Then proceed to tell the lesson.

2. You might ask a riddle such as, "I am a man who was one of the twelve spies. Ten did not trust God. Only Caleb and I thought that God would be with us. Who am I?" Then you might tell the lesson as if through the eyes of Joshua.

The Lesson: Points To Emphasize

1. God led the people to the very edge of the promised land.

2. If they had trusted God, they could have gone on into the land and settled in their new homes where they could have been happy and had everything they needed.

3. The faith of Caleb and Joshua, the two good spies, allowed them to enter the promised land.

4. The report of Caleb and Joshua, demonstrated faith in God contrasted with the report of the other ten spies.

5. The Israelites demonstrated a weak faith and sinned by believing the report of the ten faithless spies.

6. The Israelites were punished by not ever being allowed to enter the promised land. They wandered for forty years and died in the wilderness.

7. Caleb and Joshua were rewarded by being allowed to enter the promised land.

Reinforcing Activities

1. *Finger Playing:*

Twelve men went to spy in Canaan.

Ten were bad. (Hold ten fingers up followed by two thumbs down.)

Two were good. (Hold up one finger on each hand followed by two thumbs up.)

What do you think they saw in Canaan? (Hold hands over eyes as if shielding the sun.)

Ten were bad. (Repeat as above.) Two were good. (Repeat.)

Some saw giants big and strong. (Hold hand high above head, then make a muscle with arm.)

Some saw grapes with clusters long. (Hold arm out as if a pole and use other hand pulling down as if there were a long cluster of grapes.)

Twelve men went to spy in Canaan.

Ten were bad. Two were good. (Repeat as above.)

2. *Role Playing.* Allow the children to act out the lesson.

3. *Memory Verse.* Using the game suggested in lesson one (or any other method you prefer), teach the memory verse.

4. *Singing.* Sing "Anywhere with Jesus." Teach not only the tune of the song, but concentrate on the meaning of the words. If the Israelites had faith to trust God and go anywhere, they would have entered the promised land much sooner than they did.

5. *Flannel Graph.* Tell the lesson by use of a flannel graph. Help the children see as well as hear the lesson and they will remember much more.

Application

We must trust God and obey all of His commandments to enter our promised land, Heaven. We cannot only obey those commands that suit us; all of God's commandments must be learned and obeyed. As children, we are to obey our parents, respect the authority of our teachers and the government, providing the government does not tell us to live in a way contradictory to the way God would have us to live. We find God's commands in the revelation of His word, the Bible. We can learn about the Bible by attending worship services, Bible class and by reading it for ourselves. The use of pictures to represent these ideas mounted on a bulletin board to be discussed during the application portion of the lesson can help you reinforce the points of each individual idea. Depending on the maturity of your students, you could also go into the steps of obedience to the gospel as these are surely the first commands of God to be obeyed in order to become a Christian.

Visual Display

Bulletin Board

Do We Obey God As Did The

Two Spies?	Or	Ten Spies?
Attend Worship		Argue
Sing		Complain
Pray		Lie
Obey Parents		Cheat
Obey God		Fight

In-Class Worksheets

Worksheet 1:

1. Joshua, Caleb.

2-6. For questions 2-6, have the students write the answers in the cluster of grapes.

7-9. Giants, A plentiful land.

10-12. Obeying parents, attending worship, studying Bible, telling others of God, etc.

Korah's Rebellion
Num. 16-21
Lesson Aims

1. Instill a love for God as the planner for their lives and a deep trust in His ability to do what is best for them.

2. Contrast Moses as God's meek, chosen vessel with Korah, Satan's tool.

3. Emphasize how many were led astray by Korah and how God dealt with them.

Preclass Activity

1. Help each child place the Arabah rift valley on their attendance chart. Draw a diagram on the board that shows the geology of the area. Explain that in this area the surface of the ground is hard and crusty, but right below the surface there are lakes of liquid mud. God caused the earth to open up and swallow those wicked men.

2. Review with the puzzle map the locations and happenings of previous lessons.

Review Session

1. Repeat the fingerplay from lesson two.

2. Ask one of the children to tell what the spies saw. Then ask another one to tell what they told the people. Finally ask a third child to tell how the people reacted and what was the result.

Approach to the Lesson

1. You might ask if any of the children have ever been in an earthquake. Dramatize what it would be like for any who have not experienced it. Refer back to the diagram used in the pre-class activity. Tell how scary it must have been to those watching the day God caused the earth to open up and swallow some wicked men.

2. Another approach would be to ask the children if they have ever felt jealous. We all have at times. God does not want us to be jealous because it can only get us into trouble. Korah was jealous of Moses and he started some trouble. It cost him his life.

The Lesson: Points to Emphasize

1. Moses was a good leader always doing things as God wanted them done. Emphasize his meekness he was not afraid but controlled his power. Moses was never jealous or conceited.

2. Korah was not satisified to do his own work, but wanted to have honor. He was jealous.

3. Korah stirred up others and encouraged them to do wrong.

4. Moses still did not do wrong.

5. The wicked were punished.

Reinforcing Activities

1. *Vocabulary*. Write the words "censer," "meek" and "rebellion" on the board. Discuss each one and its tie with our lesson today.

2. *Comparison*. Write 14,700 ÷ 250 = 14,950 (plus Korah and his family plus Abiram and Dathan and their families) These died as a result of his jealously. Check in your area for a well-known town, or stadium, or school, with a population or seating capacity of approximately 15,000 people. Tell the children to imagine that entire stadium full of people being killed. This is the consequence of sin.

3. *Singing*. Sing "Angry Words Oh Let Them Never." Then discuss the meaning of each verse. Compare this song with Korah's jealous attitude and how he also got his friends all stirred up. Talk about why this is wrong.

4. *Praying*. Word a fervent prayer asking God to give us strength not to be jealous and not to cause our friends to share our bad feelings.

5. *Discussion*. Talk about ways to overcome bad feelings and the importance of bridling our tongues.

Application

Just as God punished the wicked during the time of Moses, He will punish those who are wicked today. The earth will not open up and swallow us, but we are assured that a day of judgment will come. Korah tried to change God's plan. Some men try to change God's plan today by adding things that can not be found in God's Word. We are warned not to listen to these false teachers or, like Korah's friends, we will be punished for not believing God.

Visual Display

Bulletin Board:

Teaching For Doctrine The Commandments Of Men
Sing   Or   Play?
Where are our hearts?

Preachers   Or   Bus?
Where is our money?

In-Class Worksheets:

Across	Down
3. Korah	1. Moses
4. Leaders	2. Jealous
6. Censers	5. Sinned

The second worksheet is a review game. To advance, the individual child must answer questions worth a certain number of squares. Cut out markers from construction paper so that each child can keep their place.

5 Point Questions.

1. What was the tent of worship called?
2. Who were the sons of Anak?
3. Who led the rebellion against God and Moses?

4 Point Questions.

1. Name the mountain where God gave the law to Moses.
2. Name the two good spies.
3. How did God punish Korah, Dathan, and Abiram?

3 Point Questions.

1. What were the people worshipping when Moses came down from the mountain?
2. How were the people punished for believing the ten bad spies?
3. How were the 250 men punished who followed Korah?

2 Point Questions.

1. How did God lead the people as they wandered?
2. What did the spies see in Canaan?
3. How were the people punished who blamed Moses for Korah's death?

How Moses Left His People
Num. 20:2-13; 27:12-23; Deut. 34

Lesson Aims

1. Show through the example of Moses that God requires obedience. The only one who never disobeyed God was Christ.

2. Throuh Moses' example emphasize the dedication of a true servant of God. His dying wish was that the people he loved might obey and love God.

Preclass Activity

Add Mt. Nebo to the puzzle map. Let the children add Mt. Nebo to their attendance charts. If time permits, take all the pieces down and let them work the puzzle reviewing people and happenings that occurred at each place.

Review

On a bulletin board have one column on the right with answers and another on the left with questions. Next to each question, have a large headed pin with enough string attached to reach the answer. Allow the children to come up one at a time and match the string with the correct answers.

	Questions	Answers
1.	What country were the Israelites camped in?	Balak
2.	What was the king's name?	Moab
3.	Why was he afraid of the Israelites?	God
4.	What did he decide to do about it?	Curse
5.	Why did Balaam want to go?	Blessed
6.	Balaam's _____ talked to him.	News of the Amorites
7.	An _____ stood in front of Balaam's donkey.	Angel
8.	Balaam _____ the Israelites.	Send for Balaam
9.	Balak wanted Balaam to _____ the Israelites.	Donkey
10.	Balaam could only say what _____ told to him.	Promise of riches

An Approach To The Lesson

1. Sing verse three of "Sweet Hour Of Prayer." Tell how this verse refers to how Moses died and left his people. Compare the promised land of Canaan to our promised land of Heaven.

2. Teach the memory verse. Explain how Moses was a gret prophet. Review all the moments of triumph. Then with sadness and seriousness tell of the incident at the Waters of Meribah resulting in Moses dying without being able to enter the Promised land.

The Lesson: Points To Emphasize

1. Mention that the Israelites were camped just across the Jordan River from the Promised Land.

2. Be certain that the children understand that the Pro-

mised Land and Canaan are the same country and why it was called the Promised Land.

3. Discuss Moses, his great work as a leader, his trust in God and how much he tried to keep the people from disobeying God.

4. Mention the one record of Moses' disobedience.

5. Remind the class that Joshua was chosen as their new leader. He was one of the good spies.

6. Describe what Moses saw from the top of Mt. Pisgah as he looked over into Canaan.

Reinforcing Activities

1. *Slides.* If available to you, there are some beautiful slides of the Bible lands. How effective your lesson could be if the children could actually see Mt. Nebo and a view across the Jordan River taken from Mt. Pisgah.

2. *Role Playing.* After showing the slides, have the children role play Moses' disobedience, his last talk to the people and his final climb to Mt. Pisgah.

3. *Praying.* Word a fervent prayer asking God to guide us as He did His children during the wandering period, thanking Him for taking care of us and asking God that we might have the faith of Moses.

Application

God provides for us. Today we are promised food and clothing while here on earth. We also have a Promised Land that we are journeying toward, but it is a spiritual land — Heaven. God required obedience from Moses in order to enter the Promised Land. Moses disobeyed and was punished. The old law was very hard to keep. No one could keep it perfectly. Along with a new Promised Land God has given us a new law which makes provisions for our mistakes. God still requires obedience; but if we make a mistake, He will forgive us if we repent and obey.

Visual Displays
Bulletin Board

God Says Obey

Hear — Read Bible-Preachers-Teachers

Believe — Believe in God and His promises

Repent — Be sorry for sin & *quit* doing it.

Confess — Jesus as Christ, God's son.

Be Baptized — Buried in water for forgiveness of sin.

Stay Faithful — Continue to study, always trying to please God.

41

In-Class Worksheets

The case study is designed to make the children see the necessity of complete obedience. The fact that God requires children to obey their parents is a proving ground for future obedience to the authority of God. Stress that Mike's mom depended on him to help her. There were more pleasurable things to do, but Mike needed to set a priority. His attitude was poor and in his haste he forgot the milk. He did not obey his mom and because of his half-hearted effort, the family had no hot bread to eat at dinner that night. Forgetting the milk may seem like a small thing but the lack of one ingredient can spoil a recipe. Our service to God must be wholehearted. We may not understand God's "recipe" just as Mike did not realize what all his mom had in mind, but we must always be ready to obey God's commandments with willing hearts and be diligent lest we forget any of His commands.

Worksheet 2: Altar, Balaam, Caleb, Donkey, Earth, Figs, God, High Place or Hill, Idols, Jordan, Korah, Law and Moses.

Using the answers from the A.B.C. exercise have the student's circle the words in the word hunt. A completed puzzle is shown below for your convience.

Word Hunt

Rahab Helps The Spies
Joshua 2
Lesson Aims

1. Each student should learn through the example of Rahab that the word of God is powerful and that He uses His people to spread His word. (Rahab had heard of miraculous happenings and of their conquest of other nations.)

2. Emphasize that God provides a way to save those who believe in Him and obey Him.

Preclass Activity

1. Help each child place the city of Jericho on their attendance chart maps.

2. Write the vocabulary words on the board. Ask if they can remember another time the Israelites sent spies into Canaan? Review the lesson of the twelve spies. Ask if they can remember another time the Israelites were pursued (chased) by someone? Recap the events of the crossing of the Red Sea.

Review

On three by five cards write the following words; tabernacles, Joshua and Caleb, Korah, Abiram, Dathan, Balaam, Balak, Moses, Mt. Nebo (Pisgah), Arabah Rift Valley and the Jordan River. Ask the children if the card you are holding up is a person, place or thing. Then ask if the children can tell you something about it. You might want to go into greater detail when reviewing Moses and his death as this was the last lesson taught and has not been reviewed before.

An Approach To The Lesson

1. You might approach the lesson by asking a riddle such as, "I am a woman who lives in Jericho. I risked my life to help the two Israelites spies. Who am I?"

2. Another approach would be to hold up a piece of red yarn telling the children to imagine this as a strong red rope (the kind Rahab might have used to help the spies escape down the wall). Ask the children if they remember that Rahab and the spies agreed to use the scarlet rope to identify her house, so her family would not be destroyed, when the Israelites attacked.

Points To Emphasize In The Lesson

1. The Israelites were camped just across the Jordan from the Promised Land.

2. Jericho was protected by great walls.

3. Rahab was friendly and helpful because of her belief that God has done great things for the Israelites.

4. Stress how Rahab helped the spies to escape.

5. Emphasize the promise of the spies to Rahab.

Reinforcing Activities

1. *Activity Table.* On an activity table have several building blocks. Help the children build a wall similar to that which would have surrounded Jericho. Hang your red yarn from one of the windows. Review the agreement made between the spies and Rahab. Her salvation depended upon two things: she must have her entire family in her house and she must have her house marked by the red rope.

2. *Singing.* Sing "I'm Not Ashamed To Own My Lord." Discuss, after singing, how Rahab had chosen God over the idols that the people in Jericho worshipped. She was not afraid to own her Lord.

3. *Map.* Bring a real map of the Bible Lands into the class. Show the children how their attendance charts are simplified, but do actually show the same areas. Point out the Jordan River, Canaan, the Mediterranean Sea and Jericho. Show how Jericho was a strategic city, located almost in the center of Canaan.

Application

God has provided a way for us to receive salvation from destruction. Just like the city of Jericho of old was totally destroyed, so will our dwelling place (the earth) be destroyed. God provided a way of escape for Rahab because she had faith and followed instructions (obeyed). If Rahab had disobeyed and either not have had her family under her roof, or failed to tie the scarlet rope outside her window, she and her family would have been lost. We are required to obey God today through baptism, and it is during the baptism that we are "marked" spiritually by the blood of Christ.

Visual Displays
Bulletin Board

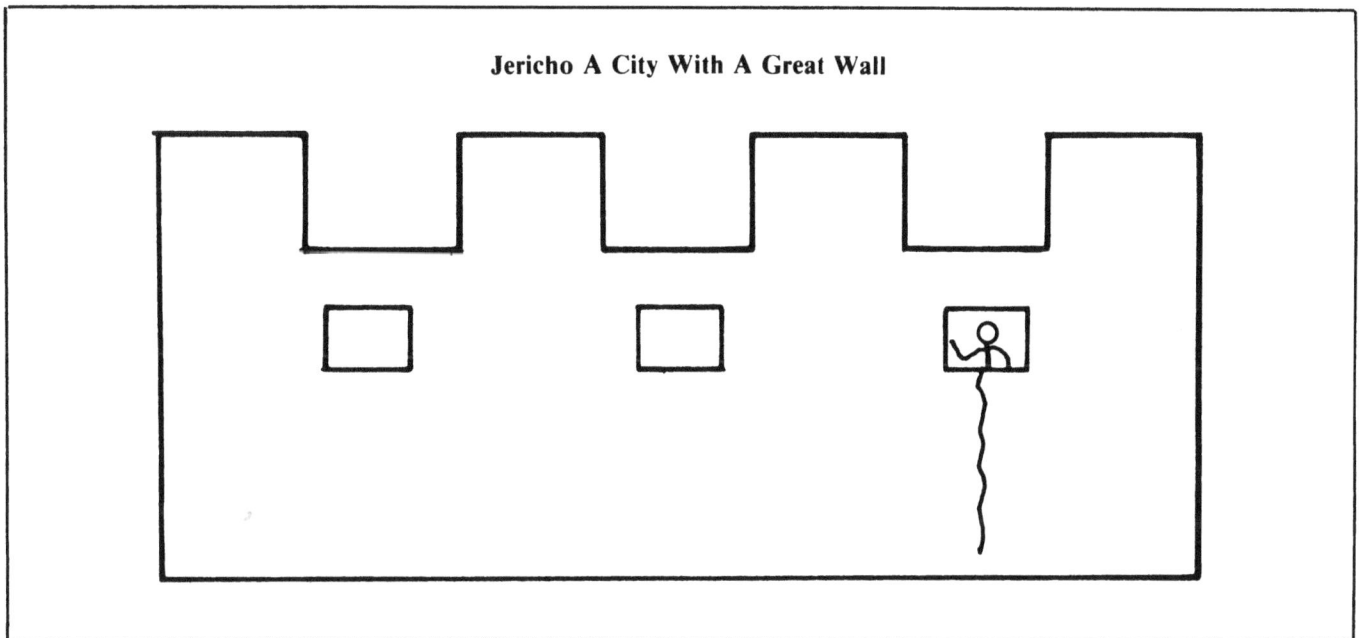

Jericho A City With A Great Wall

In-Class Worksheet

1. The geography drill is designed to help the students place cities and areas in the proper perspective and to associate the people and events that occurred there. You may use it as a test or work it together in class.

2. The wall of Jericho is designed to help the students understand the strength of the Israelites and God's providence in breaking down that great wall.

Be sure to explain to the children that each name represented an entire tribe of people. God had blessed each and every one of the Israelite tribes with many children and by this time they were indeed a very great nation of people.

Entering The Promised Land
Joshua 3-4
Lesson Aims

1. Each student should understand that God's land promise to Abraham has been fulfilled by conquering Canaan.

2. Impress upon the children God's power over the laws of nature.

3. Familiarize the students with that portion of Old Testament history relating to the conquest of Canaan.

4. Discuss how the setting up of stones and the Lord's supper are both memorials.

Preclass Activity

1. Have each child place an arrow over the point on the Jordan River where the Israelites crossed.

2. Find pictures that represent well known "memorials," such as the Washington Monument, Statue of Liberty, or a statue of a former president. Tell of the history relating to these memorials or monuments. Define a memorial. Explain that God commanded that a memorial of stones be erected as a teaching tool to remind the Israelites of His great protection and power.

Review

Tape the following questions under each chair. Have each student reach under their chair and answer his question.

1. How many spies went to Jericho?

2. Who helped them? Why?

3. What promise did the spies make to Rahab?

4. What did Rahab have to do in order to save herself and her family?

5. How did Rahab help the spies escape?

An Approach To The Lesson

1. You might ask a question like, "Have you ever gone on a vacation and brought home a souvenir to remind you of the good time you had? Well, in today's lesson we find the children of Israel setting up a monument to remind them of a very special time."

2. You could walk over to a map and point out the city of Adam which is about sixteen miles upstream from where the children of Israel crossed the Jordan. Read Josh. 3:13-17. Explain that the stopping of the water was a miracle performed by God. In 1927, earth tremors caused a landslide of the high clay river banks in Adam. The result was that for over twenty-one hours, the Jordan River was dammed up. Emphasize that the landslide was a natural phenomenon, but the crossing of the Jordan by the Israelites was a miraculous parting of the waters by the power of God.

Points To Emphasize In The Lesson

1. Explain the preparation of Israel in getting ready to cross the Jordan. This included washing their clothes. See Ex. 19:10-15.

2. Mention that there was a specific procedure whereby they would follow the priests who would be carrying the Ark of the Covenant. The people were to keep a distance of two thousand cubits (approximately one-half mile) between them and the priests so they could see which way they should go.

3. Differentiate between the Ark of the Covenant and Noah's Ark.

4. Explain why the priests were instructed to stand still with the Ark of the Covenant in the midst of the Jordan. Explain the similarities of function of the Ark of the Covenant with Moses' staff in reference to the crossing of the Red Sea.

5. Explain what the memorial was and what it symbolized.

6. Dramatize the grandeur of the procession mentioning the great number of people involved. Try to imagine the length of time it would have taken to accomplish this river crossing.

7. Remind the students that two and one-half tribes were to cross the Jordan dressed in battle array which had been commanded by God previously through Moses in order that they might begin the conquest of Canaan. This crossing was the fulfillment of the land promise given to Abraham by God (Gen. 12:1).

8. Instill an appreciation for the readiness of these Israelites who had been preparing for this conquest for forty years.

Reinforcing Activities

1. *Singing.* Sing, "On Jordan's Stormy Banks I Stand." Compare their literal crossing with our spiritual crossing to our promised land, Heaven.

2. *Bulletin Board.* See visual displays. The contents of the ark, the tablets of stone which had the Ten Commandments written on them, the pot of manna that never spoiled, and Aaron's rod that budded were all memorials to remind them of (1) their law, (2) God's provision in the wilderness, and (3) God's chosen priests or leaders.

3. *Pictures.* Locate a picture of an Israelite dressed in battle array to show how impressive the forty thousand must have looked at the crossing. Reference books on customs would reveal this sort of information.

4. *Communion.* Borrow the plate and a tray of cups or have a picture representing these things. Explain that this is a memorial that we observe in our worship today. Instruct the children in proper conduct during the communion.

Application

God throughout history has set up memorials to be observed by His people. The Lord's Supper is the memorial for Christians to observe. Once each week, on the first day of the week, we come to this memorial to remember the greatest event in all the world — the resurrection of Jesus from the dead! Just as He came forth from the graves, we will also be raised. He has promised to come back from Heaven and take us with Him. We must obey Him so that we will be one of His when He comes back.

Primary children can be taught the meaning of the Lord's Supper. They can be trained to think about Christ's sacrifice as the communion is being observed. They can understand that this is for older persons who are members of the church. Children who love Jesus and know the facts of His life and crucifixion should be remembering Him when they observe others partaking of this memorial.

Visual Display

Bulletin Board

Contents of the Ark

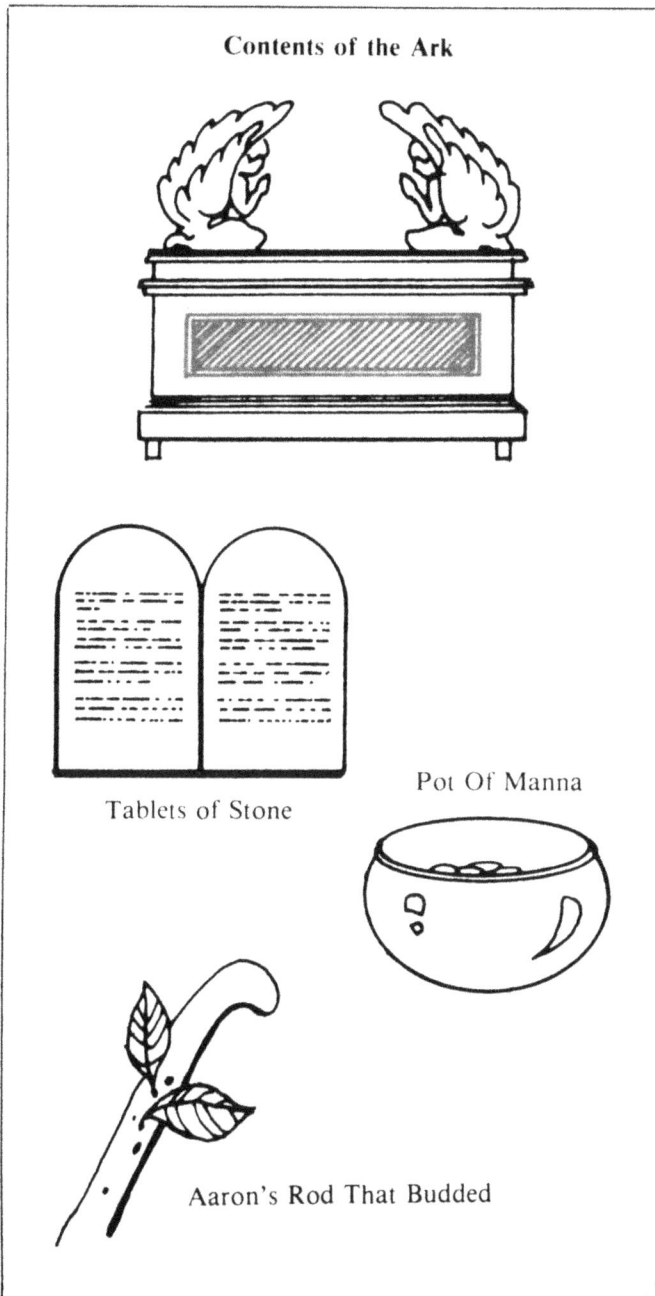

Tablets of Stone

Pot Of Manna

Aaron's Rod That Budded

How The Israelites Captured Jericho
Joshua 5-6
Lesson Aims

1. After studying this lesson, the student should understand how God's will is accomplished even over seemingly invincible forces.

2. Instill within the children a deep faith that God will be with His people, if they have a desire to be on His side.

Preclass Activity

1. Make walls of Jericho out of cardboard. This can be done by taking sides of large boxes and drawing blocks with windows on them. As the children enter the room, let each one draw something on a portion of the wall. Some of the things they might draw would be a flower pot, the gate, the scarlet rope or a soldier. This wall can be used later as an aid when the children role-play the lesson.

2. Help the children place the circle from the attendance chart around the city of Jericho.

Review

Start a brief review by telling the highlights of the previous lesson. Stop and let each child continue filling in the silent places. This would be a verbal filling in of the blanks.

An Approach To The Lesson

1. Ask the children to try and recall a movie they might have seen where there was a great battle-like Ben Hur. Discuss how most battles begin with much fighting, shouting, swords klinking or, in later times, guns shooting. Then tell them how different it was when God's people captured the first city in Canaan. The only noise was the constant blasts of trumpets.

2. Sing "Onward Christian Soldiers." Discuss how Joshua and all of his army had to depend on God. They never could have taken so great a city as Jericho without God's help and protection.

Points To Emphasize In The Lesson

1. Dramatize how happy the Israelites must have felt on reaching their destination at last. Mention the plan, order of march, etc.

2. Describe the function of their camp in Gilgal. They remained there during the time they were conquering the wicked people in Canaan.

3. Mention that the manna ceased in Gilgal.

4. Stress that Jericho ordinarily would have been a very hard city to capture.

5. Relate Joshua's willingness to obey all of God's commands and his obedience to every detail of God's plan for capturing the city.

6. Describe the wonder of the event — walls falling because the people had faith in God and how He caused it to happen.

7. Mention that Rahab and her family's safety was a reward for her faith in the one God, unlike the gods her people worshipped.

Reinforcing Activities

1. *Picture*. If you have access to *Eerdman's Handbook to the Bible,* there is an excellent picture on page 210 of a "shofar" or ram's horn. Pass the book around the class and allow each child to see what the priests used, to make their nerve-racking blasts, as they compassed the city.

2. *Role-playing*. Allow the children to role-play the lesson. You can use the cardboard walls that you made during the preclass activity. Rolled pieces of construction paper can be used for the ram's horns.

3. *Bulletin Board* (see visual display). Put on the whole armor of God. See Eph. 6:11-17. Compare these scriptures with the lack of weapons used by the Israelites in capturing Jericho.

Application

Today we fight a spiritual battle. To enter our promised land, we must arm ourselves with the word of God. Use the bulletin board to teach this to the children.

Visual Display

Bulletin Board

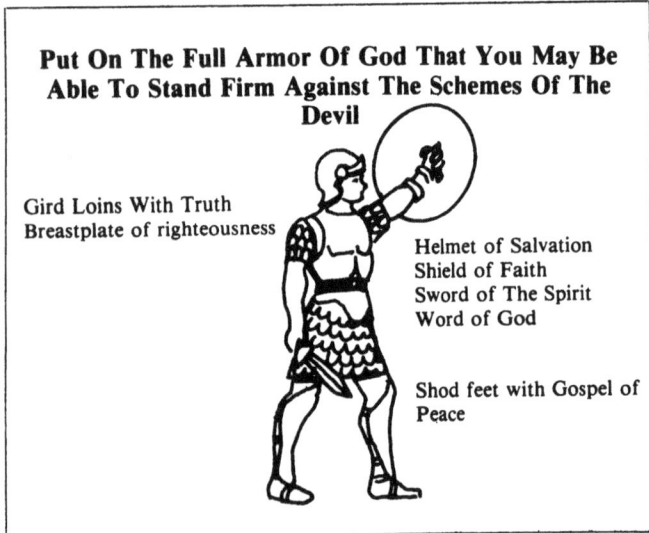

Put On The Full Armor Of God That You May Be Able To Stand Firm Against The Schemes Of The Devil

Gird Loins With Truth
Breastplate of righteousness

Helmet of Salvation
Shield of Faith
Sword of The Spirit
Word of God

Shod feet with Gospel of Peace

In-Class Worksheets

The Vocabulary drills are designed to review both the words and the lessons from which they took place. Help the children with the words and their definitions and fill them in a class exercise rather than as a test.

1.	tabernacle	D	6.	carcasses	H
2.	wilderness	E	7.	censer	N
3.	camp	G	8.	meek	B
4.	spy	A	9.	rebellion	M
5.	murmur	J	10.	angel	C

11.	blessing.	K	16.	overflow.	F
12.	curse	R	17.	sanctify	L
13.	prophet	P	18.	compassed.	O
14.	pursue	S	19.	shofar	Q
15.	memorial	I			

Below are listed the answers to the crossword puzzle in the student's book.

Across	Down
2. shofar	1. Rahab
5. Canaan	3. fell
7. obeyed	4. Jericho
	6. seven

How Sin Lost A Battle
Josh. 7-8

Lesson Aims

1. Teach the consequences of sin and how many times your sin affects the lives of others.

2. Emphasize that stealing is wrong.

3. Introduce the thought that God is only with those nations that obey Him.

Preclass Activity

1. Cut some pictures from a magazine of things the children would probably enjoy having (toys, cookies, etc.). As the children enter the room let each one choose a picture of the thing they would like to have the most. Ask them if they were sure no one was watching them and they thought they could get the item home would they be tempted to just take one? Stress the following reasons this would be wrong: (a) God would know even if no one else ever found out. (b) Like Achan, where could you use it without anyone knowing? You would have to hide it and then what good would it do you? (c) The Bible tells us it is wrong to steal. (d) There is joy in working for something and obtaining it honorably. (e) If you get caught, you will be punished. If not, you will eventually be punished by God if you have not repented and been forgiven by the time you die. (f) Someone will have to pay for the item. If many things are stolen from a store, the store then must raise its prices to be able to stay in business.

2. Help the children place Ai on their attendance charts.

Review

Discuss the highlights of the capture of Jericho as a review and also lay groundwork for today's lesson.

An Approach To The Lesson

1. Referring back to the pictures used in the preclass activity, you might tell the children that seeing something and wanting it very much is a feeling people have felt ever since Adam and Eve. Explain that today's lesson tells about a man who was an Israelite who saw some things he wanted so badly that he disobeyed God and took them.

2. Bring a sleeveless coat, a gold bracelet (preferably one which can be stretched out to represent a bar of gold) and some silver coins to class. Hold them up and show the children how items like these tempted a man named Achan to sin.

Points To Emphasize In The Lesson

1. This battle was lost because one of them had disobeyed God. They could not overcome their enemies when they did not obey God.

2. Achan could not hide from God and was punished by God.

3. Achan sinned in wanting something that did not belong to him. He knew what God had said concerning these things.

4. God knew who the guilty man was and assisted Joshua in finding him.

5. God blessed the Israelites after the sinful person was removed.

Reinforcing Activities

1. *Role Playing.* Bring a sheet or bedspread to class and drape it over some chairs to make Achan's tent. Hide the sleeveless coat (used in the lesson approach), gold bar bracelet and the coins under a piece of brown construction paper to represent them being buried. The children can throw rocks of black construction paper to stone Achan. Retell the lesson encouraging each child to put real feeling into their role.

2. *Singing.* Sing "Yield Not To Temptation," stressing that we are all tempted at different times and with God's help we can overcome these feelings.

3. *Puzzle Map Drill.* Review on your large puzzle map the location of Ai as compared to Jericho. By now the children should be able to easily place the pieces on the proper areas.

4. *Memory Verse.* Teach the memory verse discussing the consequences of sin.

Application

We learn through Achan that stealing is wrong. Sometimes when we do wrong it not only hurts us, but others. Just like God was not with Isreal because of one man's sin, how can we expect God to be with our nation if so many are sinning?

We must study God's word, pray, attend services and tell others. Our prayers should include asking God to be with our leaders, both national and spiritual, as well as asking for strength for ourselves.

Visual Displays

(See Next Page)

Teach Us To Pray

For Ourselves

For The Preacher

For The Elders

For The President

For Other Christians

For Congress

For Foreign Leaders

For Teachers

For Parents

For The Lost

Joshua Teaches God's Law
Deut. 27:11-26; Josh. 8

Lesson Aims

1. Teach the importance of studying God's laws so that we may obey them.

2. Show through the example of Joshua that we must obey exactly those commandments given to us.

3. Familiarize the students with some of the Old Testament methods of worship and teach that God no longer requires us to worship that way today.

Preclass Activity

1. Assist the children in placing their attendance sticker on their maps.

2. Have the Ten Commandments written on separate 3" x 5" cards. As the children come in, let each one take one of the cards. On the bulletin board have an outline of the tablets of stone. Let each child place his commandment on the board and then discuss its meaning.

Review Session

1. Ask a riddle, "I am a man who stole some silver coins, a bar of gold and a beautiful coat from Jericho. I was punished by being stoned to death. Who Am I?"

2. After the children answer the riddle, ask some questions to review the lesson from last week.

An Approach To The Lesson

1. Teach the memory verse. Discuss the meaning of the word "worship." This could easily lead into a discussion of how the Israelites worshipped God differently than we do. Then proceed to tell the lesson.

2. Using your bulletin board from the preclass activity, explain that the Ten Commandments are part of God's old law. This was the law written to the Israelites and was in effect until Jesus died on the cross. The lesson today tells some of the ways the people worshipped then. Emphasize that even though we worship differently today, we do so because God changed His law. He gave a new law through His Son. It is just as important for us today to follow God's commands as it was for Joshua and the Israelites.

Points To Emphasize In The Lesson

1. The Israelites were still at Gilgal and had captured two important cities. The way was opened for them to go further into Canaan.

2. They had been told by Moses long before that they should have this worship service.

3. The people needed to have God's laws taught to them again to help them obey them.

4. They were worshipping God, learning His laws, and promising again to serve Him.

5. Compare their worship to ours. We have one day a week when God has told us to meet for a worship service.

6. We will be happy if we obey God in what He tells us to do; we will be unhappy if we disobey God just as were the Israelites.

7. In our worship service, we hear God's word read and taught also.

8. It was for the benefit of the Israelites to worship God and learn His laws. It is for our benefit also to worship God in the way He has told us to worship. Is is for our good that we study the Bible as it was for the Israelite benefit to study God's law.

Reinforcing Activities

1. *Puzzle Map.* Have the children work with the large puzzle map. Concentrate on retracing the steps from the crossing of the Jordan, then to Jericho, Ai, and for today's lesson Mt. Ebal.

2. *Altar building.* Build an altar out of cardboard stones. Have the children place the Ten Commandments on it.

3. *Singing.* Sing, "Give Me The Bible." After singing, discuss how today we have God's word. God chose not to reveal any portion of His will for us on tablets of stone.

4. *Praying.* Word a fervent prayer asking God for strength similar to that of Joshua who obeyed all of God's commands exactly.

Application

We must be diligent to obey God always. We can not take portions of His word and obey only those things that please us. One command which God gives us is to assemble on the first day of the week. During this assembly we are to hear God's word (preaching), partake of the memorial feast (Lord's Supper), sing praises, offer prayer, and give of our means. This is how God wants us to worship today.

Visual Displays
Bulletin Board

How We Worship Today

Preaching

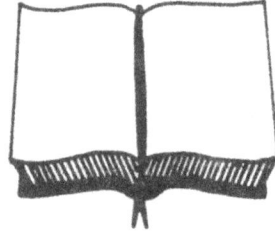

Bible

Singing

Communion

Prayer

Giving

How The Gibeonites Tricked Joshua
Josh. 9
Lesson Aims

1. Teach the mistakes we make when we fail to pray to God regarding important decisions.

2. Discuss the extremes people without God will go to in deceiving others.

Preclass Activity

1. Place Gibeon on attendance chart map. Review its location on the large map.

2. On an activity table you could have some old worn out clothing. As the children enter the room you might ask them how the clothing pertains to our lesson today. Guide the children into thinking of the lesson as soon as they enter the door.

Review

Start a brief narrative of how Joshua built an altar. Stop and allow each child to pick up where you left off until the lesson from last class is reviewed sufficiently.

An Approach To The Lesson

1. Begin dressing in the old clothes from the activity table. Tell the lesson as if you were a Gibeonite. Stress the fear that you will be killed instantly by Joshua and his men if recognized. Discuss their cunning in not mentioning the defeat of Jericho and Ai, pretending their old bread had been fresh when they left and their clothing new.

2. Walk over to the puzzle map; talk of Gibeon's location (only three day's journey). Stress how the news of the victories of the Israelites have reached all the surrounding cities and how the people were afraid.

Points To Emphasize In The Lesson

1. Discuss the appearance of the strangers.

2. Tell of their reason for coming to Joshua.

3. Describe the way they deceived Joshua and that this was wrong.

4. Reveal Joshua's mistake in not finding out first what God wanted him to do in this case.

5. Explain why the Gibeonites were afraid of the Israelites.

6. Mention the fact that the Gibeonites were punished for deceiving the Israelites. (They were made slaves.)

7. Emphasize the fact that the Israelites later had trouble because they made an agreement of peace with these people and God had told them not to make peace with any of the wicked people in Canaan.

8. Stress that Joshua kept his promise to the people of Gibeon.

Reinforcing Activities

1. *Role playing.* This lesson is an excellent one for the children to role play. Be sure those who play the Gibeonites realize the craftiness of their deceit.

2. *Matching game.* On a bulletin board have one column headed Gibeonites and another headed Israelites. Write pertinent information regarding each group on "three by five cards." Read the statement from each card and allow any child who can answer to come up and place the card under the proper column. This game can also be used as a review for the next class session.

3. *Praying.* We should stress prayer in this lesson as that is our way of putting important decisions in God's hands. Review with the children, who and for what, we should pray. Ask each one to make a list of what they want to pray about this week. Tell them to look at the list right before saying their prayers. Ask them to tell you at the next class meeting if the lists helped them remember some of the things they might otherwise have forgotten.

4. *Memory verse.* Explain the consequences of lying.

Application

This lesson has two very important applications. The first is the people of the world are often deceitful. Sometimes for one reason or another they will try to trick you and use you. The Christian must always study God's word so he will be able to discern right from wrong.

The second point that we should not overlook is that we should not make important decisions hastily. We need to pray and meditate about the matter. Only after such, will God lead us to a wise decision on the matter. We must trust that He will do so. Our faithful attitude is important.

Visual Display

Bulletin Board

Joshua failed to ask God first. We know what God wants us to do by

Study

Prayer

The Day The Sun Stood Still
Josh. 10

Lesson Aims

1. Teach the power of God and His providence in caring for His children through the miraculous event of the long day.

2. Instill a faith in the children that God will protect and provide for them.

Preclass Activity

1. Place Jerusalem on attendance charts and large map.

2. On an activity table, place a globe with a "Tensor light" shining on it. Demonstrate to the students how the earth rotates around the sun and also on its axis. This is how the normal passing of time is measured. Show what would happen if this movement stopped. The sun (or light) would stay upon whichever spot it happened to be shining. Ask the children if they can think of anyone with enough power to make that happen. Talk about the power of God, how He made the earth and all that is in it. He would be the only one with enough power to make the sun stand still.

Review

See the game from lesson eleven. This would serve as an excellent review.

An Approach To The Lesson

1. You might say something like, "Remember the demonstration of how the earth rotates around the sun?" Walk over to the activity table and repeat the motion of the earth's rotation. "Our lesson today is about a time when God made the sun stand still so that Joshua and the Israelites would have enough time to finish a battle! This is how it happened. . . ."

2. Another approach would be to go directly from the review of how the Gibeonites tricked Joshua into the fact that as a result of their treaty the Israelites had to fight a really big battle.

Points To Emphasize In The Lesson

1. Stress the fear that all the surrounding kings had because the Israelites and the mighty Gibeonites were now allies.

2. Mention that they had good cause to fear. They could have learned, as Rahab did, to believe in and serve the true God instead of idols.

3. Emphasize that though five great armies were united against God's army, the five could not win. Even though all the people in the land might have banded together, they could have never conquered God's people. God would not allow that to happen.

4. Dramatize the most unusual and powerful way in which God helped the Israelites by making the sun stand still, lengthening the day and sending large hailstones from Heaven.

5. Bring to remembrance that never before or since has the sun stood still.

6. Stress that the reason God wanted the Israelites to destroy those people was because they were so very wicked and would not serve Him. If the Israelites lived among them, they would soon influence the Israelites to do the wicked things they were doing.

7. Emphasize that we must shun evil and overcome temptations. We must not have as our close friends those who are evil for they might influence us to do wrong.

Reinforcing Activities

1. *Pictures.* Locate pictures of warriors dressed appropriately for the times and show them to the children. You could point out the usual advantage of having a larger army and more weapons, but stress that, in this instance, God was with the smaller army. One method God used to help equal the number was by sending a shower of large hailstones which stoned to death many of the men of the opposing army. Define hail and locate a picture if possible to further reinforce this point.

2. *Memory verse game.* Teach the children the memory verse by allowing the individual students to write it, one word at a time, upon the board. Stress God's love and protection by relating the memory verse to the lesson.

3. *Singing.* Sing, "Anywhere With Jesus." Teach how the Israelites were victorious in battle even against great odds because God was with them. Apply this same principal to us, that if we are willing to let Jesus lead our lives, we have nothing to fear for He is with us.

4. *Map drill.* Using the large puzzle map review the main bodies of water and the pertinent cities and mountains for the evaluation that will be given next class period. (See the Student's Worksheet for lesson thirteen.)

Application

God helped the children of Israel win battles over very large armies because it was God's will that these sinful, idol worshippers be destroyed. He knew that if these wicked people were allowed to live among His people, that they would soon become friends. Then, God's people would start listening to them and turn away from God. We are warned today of people who do not worship God according to the way He has told us. We are told to study His word so that we can recognize evil and to pray for strength to overcome temptations. We are also told that, "evil companions corrupt good morals," showing that it is easier to do wrong than right. What is the solution? It is studying God's word, praying and choosing only as our close friends those who will encourage us to do the right thing. Then how would we ever teach unbelievers the word of God? We must realize that once we have tried to teach them and they fail to change their evil ways, we must not become too friendly with them. This is a difficult thing to teach young children, but they must be made to realize the seriousness of conformig to the world.

Visual Displays
Bulletin Board

Be Not Conformed To The World
Smoking
Gambling
Test
Cheating
Drinking
Drugs
Lying
Stealing

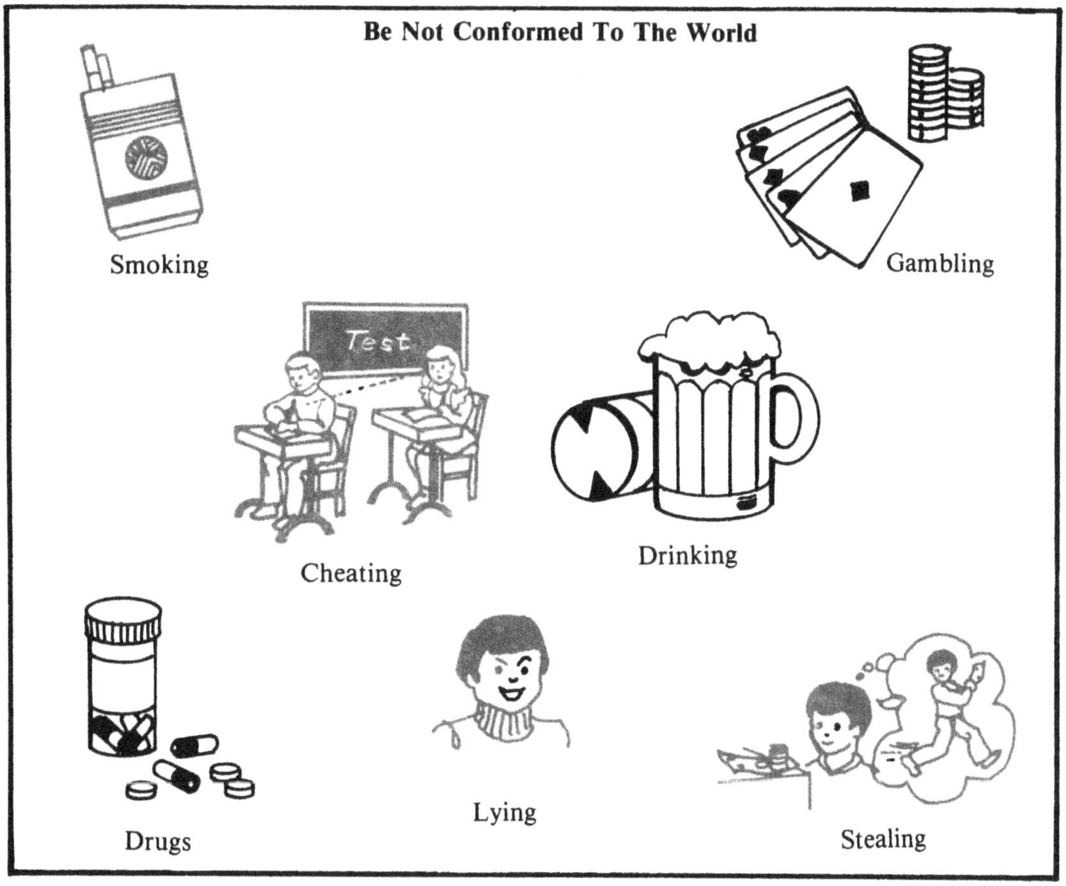

As you discuss each item you might place a large **X** made from construction paper over each picture.

The Land Of Israel
Joshua 11-24

Lesson Aims

1. Emphasize the completion of God's promise to give the land to Israel.

2. Teach the importance of continuing to serve God and remain faithful to Him.

Preclass Activity

1. Have the children list the names of the twelve tribes on their attendance chart. Help them draw an arrow to the area each inherited.

2. Review with the large puzzle map the main geographical areas to be covered on the test today.

Review

Have some questions pertaining to the last session written on papers. Number them one through nine and place them in a box. Pass the box around the room, each child answering his or her numbered question but having the questions answered consecutively since they are chronologically arranged. If they do not know the answer, they may pass the question to the next student.

1. Why did the king of Jerusalem want to kill the Gibeonites?

2. How many kings did he get to help him?

3. What did all five kings do?

4. What did the Gibeonites do when they heard that these armies were coming?

5. Tell what Joshua did when they sent him the news that the enemy was coming?

6. Why did Joshua want the day to be longer?

7. What did Joshua do to cause the daylight to last longer?

8. Why do you think God helped Joshua that way?

9. Why did God not want the Israelites to live among the wicked people in the land?

An Approach To The Lesson

1. You could walk over to your large bulletin board "puzzle map" and say something like, "The children of Israel have finally reached their promised land! They have had many battles to fight. (Point to Jericho, Ai and Gibeon.) Now God has a new plan to help them finish conquering the cities that are left . . . ." Teach the lesson from this point.

2. Another approach might be to compare tribes of Indians to the tribes of Israel. Explain that the twelve tribes of Israel were the families of the twelve original sons with Joseph's inheritance being divided between his two sons, Manasseh and Ephraim. When God had helped the Israelites conquer most of the land, He then told Joshua to divide the land among the twelve tribes.

Points To Emphasize In The Lesson

1. Stress the fame of the Israelites and how it spread through all the land. Their successes in battle were known to all the people.

2. Mention that a great army which was a combination of twelve armies tried to overcome the Israelites and could not.

3. Explain that Joshua was getting old. He had been faithful and true to God all of his life. He had worked hard to serve God.

4. Detail the dividing of the land into twelve tribes; two and one-half tribes crossed over the Jordan to have their possession on the east side.

5. Relate how it was each tribe's responsibility to get rid of the people who still remained in their portion of the inherited land.

6. Glamorize the life of Caleb, his request, his long faithful life and his reward for being one of the two good spies.

7. Emphasize that the land promise was now fulfilled. Canaan now belonged to the Israelites.

8. Tell of the moving of the tabernacle to Shiloh where it remained for several years, mentioning that it had been at Gilgal since the Israelites came into Canaan.

9. Dramatize Joshua's farewell speech.

Reinforcing Activities

1. *Memory Verse.* Teach the meaning of the memory verse stressing Joshua's farewell speech.

2. *Singing.* Sing "Guide Me, O Thou Great Jehovah." Stress how God guided the children of Israel and how He will guide us.

3. *Lesson Viewing Box.* Turn a cardboard box on its side. Cut two holes on the top and two on the bottom large enough to slip through some broom or mop handles. Use an old white sheet. Cut the width for your scenes. (Stick figures will do.) Secure the sheet on the poles with masking tape so that the scenes can be rolled back and forth. Review the lesson by turning the one or two appropriate scenes on the roll.

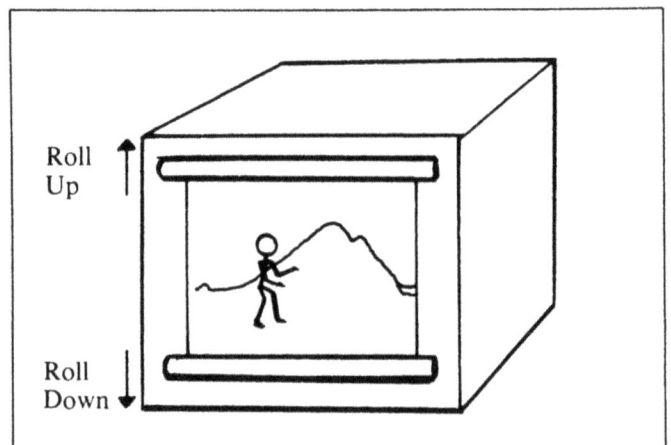

4. Test. See the In-Class Worksheet.

Application

God fulfilled His promise to give the people of Israel their land. God always fulfills His promises. He has promised us food and clothing and a home with Him when we die. We must be faithful to God and obey Him while here on earth to be eligible for these blessings.

Visual Displays

On a chalkboard, write the following list to be an aid to the students in answering the questions on their test. Be sure to cover the puzzle map on the bulletin board.

Korah	Balak
Joshua	Aaron
Moses	Achan

A New Leader For Israel
Judg. 1-3

Lesson Aims

1. The students should understand that God will bless him if he is faithful and obedient to His will.

2. The student will realize that God punished the Israelites because He loved them. Parents also punish children because they love and care for them.

3. Parents punish their children as a last resort. They are teaching them to do right. Good behavior is rewarded, and bad behavior is punished; both are done from love.

Preclass Activity

The first student to arrive can be dressed in a toga with the name Othniel pinned to it. As each child arrives, tell him briefly about the judge, his name, and what he did. Have a "Judges Ladder" prepared that can have the name of a judge added to it each class session. The top rung will read "Judges"; the additional rungs will have the judges' names on them. This lesson will be about Othniel.

Approach to the Lesson

As class begins, ask these questions, "Have you ever thought your mother or daddy was being mean to you when they punished you? Did you ever think that, if they really loved you, they would not punish you? They may have told you that they only punish you for your own good or because they love you. God treated His people the same way — punishing them when they disobeyed, because He loved them. God did not want to punish His people but He had to because they were doing wrong. Let us look at some of the things that God's people were doing that were wrong, and how God punished them.

Reinforcing Activities

1. This lesson can be effectively taught with a flannelgraph showing the Israelites disobeying (worshipping idols), then being taken captive (sad and working hard), and finally being delivered by the judge (happy people).

2. After the lesson have the student dressed as Othniel put his name (Othniel's) rung on the ladder. Each class period, have a different student for each judge.

Applications

Turn to the section in the student book entitled "Think About This" and discuss the questions. Emphasize to the students that doing only part of what one is told does not constitute obedience. Read aloud and discuss Eph. 6:2-3.

Visual Displays

In addition to the "Judges Ladder" have a bulletin board depicting what Baal and Ashteroth may have looked like. Explain that they were false gods and could do nothing. Our God can do everything and gives everything. Have pictures showing things God gave Israel and what He gives us.

Research and explain to the students the significance of the idols of Baal and Ashteroth to help them better understand what the people expected to gain from worshipping them. Emphasize how foolish this is; only a living God can provide for us; something which is lifeless and man-made cannot help a man.

Worksheets

Hand out worksheets and allow time for completion. Assist any students who need help with reading. Remember, you want the student to learn. Witholding help will not help him learn.

Fill in the Blanks: After completion have students exchange with a friend, go over the answers, and write in correct answers.

Crossword Puzzle: Answers:

Down: 1. Baal; 2. Ashteroth; 3. Idols; 4. Evil; 5. Prayed; 6. Delivered

Across: 5. Punished; 7. Canaan; 8. Othniel; 9. Agreements; 10. Disobey; 11. Judge; 12. Forty

True and False: Answers:

1. True; 2. False; 3. True; 4. False; 5. False; 6. True; 7. False; 8. False; 9. False; 10. True

Lesson Aims

1. The student will understand that, while the Israelites obeyed God, they had peace. As soon as they began to forget God, trouble came upon them. As long as we obey God, we will be happy. If we disobey, we will be more apt to have trouble.

2. The Israelites did not learn from their mistakes. Even though he sometimes does wrong and is punished, the student will realize that he needs to learn from his mistakes.

Preclass Activity

Have a toga and an "Ehud" name tag ready for the first student. You might also have a sword that has been made out of cardboard covered with aluminum foil. Talk to each child briefly about this left-handed judge.

Approach to Lesson

Begin by explaining to the class that Ehud was left-handed. The majority of the class will be right-handed and will be able to easily recognize the difference in being left-handed. Your left-handed students can do the same thing but will see the difference in the oposite. Ehud was able to defeat a wicked king with the use of his left hand.

Reinforcing Activities

After the story is told ask the class some questions to see how well they remember it. This would also be a good time to do a little review of the previous lesson. Ask them some basic questions such as: Why was God punishing the Israelites? Who was the first judge who delivered the Israelites from slavery? Who was the second judge? What was different about this judge?

Have the student dressed as Ehud place his name rung on the ladder. You may wish for this student to tell the story to the class in his own words.

Applications

The Israelites turned to worshipping idols because those around them were doing so. We must never do bad things just because we see others doing them. Worshipping and obeying God is the most important thing in life.

Worksheets

Hand out idols that are to be cut out and assembled. You will need to provide each child with a pair of blunt-tipped scissors for this. Help them put the idol together and glue or tape the bottom together to form a stand. After they are completed discuss the questions that are on the worksheet.

Hand out second worksheet and allow time for completion. Go over the answers in class. If there is not enough time to do these in class, they may be sent home for homework and brought back at the next class.

Check student books to be sure they have done their worksheets. You may want to put the "Find These Words" puzzle on a marker board or chalkboard before class and go over this in class if time permits.

Visual Displays

A bulletin board can be used depicting Ehud standing before the big, fat king holding a sword in his left hand. An additional bulletin board illustration that can be prepared and left for eight weeks can illustrate the cycle that the Israelites fell into at this time in history as shown in the introduction to this book.

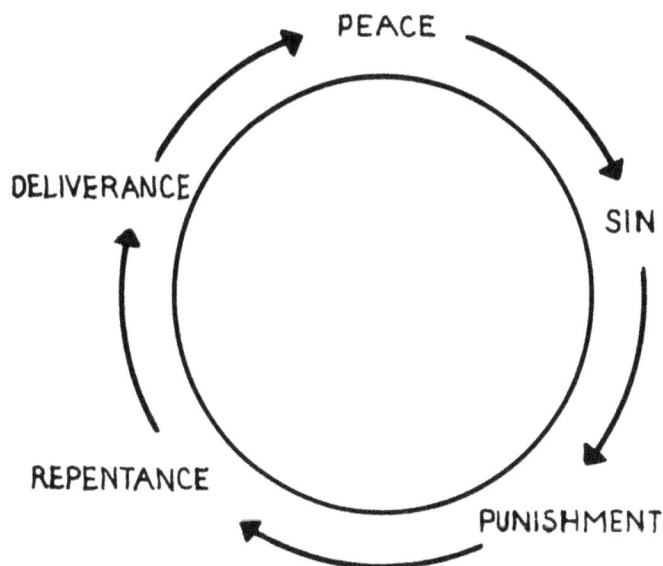

A Woman Who Was Judge
Judg. 4

Lesson Aims

1. By now the student should have a good understanding of the cycle of history which the Israelites fell into in their disobedience to God, as outlined in the introduction to this series of lessons. How the Israelites fell into idol worship, received oppression from their enemies, and were delivered should all be familiar to the students.

2. The students should be able to determine the difference between acceptable and non-acceptable behavior of the Israelites and of Christians.

Preclass Activity

The student dressed for this lesson should be a girl, if possible. Deborah was the only woman judge mentioned in the Bible. Tell the others briefly about Deborah. Tell them how her kindness and wisdom helped her people. Perhaps you can have pictures of people doing kind deeds and let them know that kindness always brings reward.

Approach to Lesson

Most of the judges rose up in the heat of a crisis. Deborah was somewhat different in that she was already well-known for her wisdom. Her people had been coming to her for some time with their problems and disputes and she had been helpful to them before any actual battle took place. She was not only a judge, but a wise consultant to her people. Take a closer look at this good woman who was judge of Israel.

Reinforcing Activities

1. This lesson can be reinforced with role-playing. You will need four students for the main characters; Deborah, Barak, Jael, and Sisera. The other students may be members of the armies. A tent can be made by draping a blanket over two chairs. Have the children tell the story as they act it out. There is no need to act out the murder scene. A simple narrative will do at that point.

2. Have the student who played Deborah place her name rung on the ladder. Above Deborah's name you will need to place a rung for Shamgar. Explain to the class that the Bible mentions several judges but we will not be studying about them because there are no details revealed about them. The Bible mentions only their names and how long they judged.

Applications

After studying these examples of God's mercy and love for His people, discuss with the class ways in which they may apply the same behavior toward every day situations in their lives. They need to be aware of ways that they can show love and mercy one for another as God shows for

them. This can include forgiving others and not seeking revenge, praying for others, etc.

Visual Displays

Have a bulletin board showing the ways in which Deborah served God such as helping her people with their problems, being their brave leader, etc., and the ways in which women today can serve God such as visiting the sick, preparing the communion, teaching Bible classes, etc.

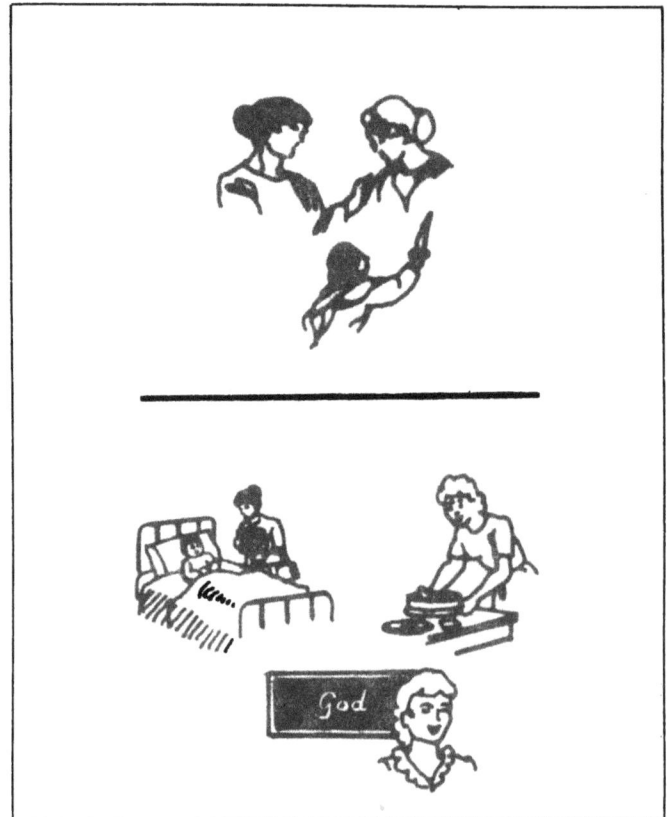

Go over again the bulletin board that depicts the cycle of the Israelites in their obedience to God. Perhaps one or two of the students can come to the board and follow the cycle giving an example of each of the steps.

Worksheets

Check the student's book to see if he has completed the home worksheets. Hand out in-class worksheets and allow time for completion. The students may check their own, or exchange, papers with a friend to check their answers.

Picture Puzzle: Deborah The Woman Judge.

Discuss the statements written on the worksheets. You may use these questions as you go over your bulletin board.

Who Does It? The class may need help with this one because of the technicalities of it. For instance, the man can take care of the baby just as much and as well as the woman. However, it truly comes under being keepers at home. In-depth study of this is not necessary for this age group.

A Brave Man Who Destroyed an Altar
Judg. 6

Lesson Aims

1. As in the previous lessons the student should understand that the Israelites brought their troubles on themselves by not worshipping God. We will bring trouble upon ourselves today if we fail to obey God.

2. After studying this lesson, the student will see the humility of Gideon and how God proved to Gideon that he should be the leader who was to deliver the Israelites. God will give us the strength we need to do the things that He wants us to do.

Preclass Activity

Dress the first student as Gideon. Perhaps you can have a fleece of wool available for the children to look at and feel. This can be a piece of fake fur found in fabric stores, or something that resembles fleece. You might also have an altar constructed to show the class what they looked like. Tell each child just a bit about these things as you will want to elaborate on them when telling the story.

Approach to Lesson

Remind the class of the past judges who we have studied and how they were eager to do as God told them to. They did not seem to need any proof that God had chosen them to lead His people. This story is about a man who was a little different in that respect. He was very skeptical and suspicious about what God wanted him to do. Let us see how God proved to him that he truly was the chosen one.

Reinforcing Activities

1. Reinforce this lesson by illustrating some of the main points of it. When you tell the part about Gideon tearing down the altar to Baal, walk over to the altar you have constructed and knock it down. You can then rebuild it as Gideon built an altar to worship God.

2. You can illustrate the test with the fleece also. This will be a bit more difficult to do because you cannot do it miraculously as God did. You will need two pieces of fleece and two pieces of artificial grass (Astroturf would do). For the first test, you can sprinkle water (perhaps from a watering can) on the fleece and keep the grass dry. You will need to explain to the class that this is not the way God makes dew but it will still help them to understand what happened. After wetting the fleece you can wring it out into a bowl just as Gideon did. Then, with the remaining pieces, illustrate the second part of the test this time by pouring the water on the grass and keeping the fleece dry. Let the children feel the difference wet and dry fleece and grass.

3. Have the student Gideon hang his name rung on the ladder, and ask him to tell the story briefly in his own words.

Applications

After illustrating these ways in which God proved to Gideon that He was the one chosen for the leader of the Israelites, discuss ways in which God has proven to us that He is the one true God, such as by the great and wonderful things which He has created for us, by sending His son to be sacrificed for our sins, etc.

Visual Displays

The altar and the fleece are excellent visual displays in themselves. A bulletin board can be made, depicting one of the scenes from this story (perhaps of Gideon wringing the dew out of the fleece).

Describe to the students how devastating the oppression of the Midianites was. This was possibly the worst oppression Israel suffered. You may be able to find some pictures illustrating the suffering of Israel in a pictorial Bible encyclopedia. The people were near starvation; herds of animals died for lack of food. As you discuss this, continue to stress the fact that the Israelites brought all of this upon themselves. Let the class know just how severely God deals with those who do not obey Him.

Worksheets

Hand out the worksheets and allow time for completion. If time does not permit the completion of all worksheets send them home with the student to do and bring back to class the next time.

Matching. Perhaps you could write this one out on the marker board to help the students see the correct answers.

True or False. False, True, False, False, False, True, True

Fill in the Blanks. 1. punished, idols; 2. grain; 3. angel, Gideon; 4. tear down, Baal; 5. sacrifice; 6. messengers; 7. fleece, wet; 8. dry, wet; dew.

How A Battle Was Won With 300 Men
Judg. 7:1-23

Lesson Aims

1. After studying this lesson, the student will know that God deserved and should receive all of the glory for all that He gives to us and all that He does for us.

2. Gideon won the battle only because he did just what God told him to do. We will win our own personal battles if we follow God's will.

Preclass Activity

Even though Gideon's name was hung on the ladder during the last class period, you may still want to dress one of the children as Gideon or perhaps dress as Gideon youself. As the children come into class, you can review a little bit about the last lesson to refresh their memories. You can tell them that this time they will learn about the battle which Gideon fought against the Midianites.

Approach to Lesson

Probably the best approach to this lesson would be to review the previous lesson to remind the class where we had left Gideon. Quiz them briefly to see how much them remember and clear up any misunderstandings they may have. Now let us see how Gideon won that battle with God's help.

Reinforcing Activities

1. This lesson can be told with a sandbox scene set up on a table. Pipe-cleaner figures can be used. You can show how Gideon's army started out very large and ended up being a very small army indeed. Of course, you cannot possibly have thousands of figures so you must scale it down to a reasonable number. Just be sure that Midian's army has quite a few more figures than Gideon's army. You can show how the Israelites surrounded the city and explain to the class how frightened the Medianites were. They can imagine themselves being awakened in the same manner and how frightened they would be. Be sure to continue to stress the fact that it was God, not the men or Gideon, who defeated the Midianites.

2. Have the student who is dressed as Gideon tell the story in his own words. If you have dressed as Gideon, ask the students some questions about the story and throw in a few questions about the previous lessons. See if they can name the judges they have studied as far without looking at the ladder. As they memorize the judges, be sure to include those who are not mentioned in our lessons.

Applications

The memory verse is a good application to our lives. We should be aware that many inanimate things can rule our lives such as money, fame, power, or even something like television. We must be careful that we do not become subject to these things. God is the one and only ruler over us, and we are subject to Him.

Visual Displays

The sandbox scene of course is a fine visual display. Perhaps you can find some pictures showing a very large army and a very small army. Explain to the class how, in ordinary circumstances, the small army would be destroyed by the larger one. This did not happen in Gideon's case because God was with them.

A bulletin board can be made showing the men drinking and lapping to let the children understand the difference. This test showed nothing of the bravery or strength of the men; it was just the way God wanted it done, so that is the way Gideon did it.

Worksheets

Hand out worksheets and let the children complete them. While they are working on them you may take this time to check their books to be sure they are doing their homework.

Crossword Puzzle: Down: 1. three hundred; 2. lapped; 3. victory; 4. army. Across: 1. trumpets; 5. Midianites; 6. locusts; 7. Gideon; 8. dream; 9. pitcher.

The Bramble King
Judg. 9:1-21

Lesson Aims

1. By this time, the student should be able to state the five-step cycle of the Israelites' obedience to God, and give an example of each step.

2. The student should realize that we cannot be bad and expect to get away with it. Abimelech and the men of Shechem paid dearly for their wickedness; we will eventually have to pay for our wrong-doing.

Preclass Activity

Abimelech was a presumptuous judge of Israel; however, we need to study about him. However, you will need to add his name and the names of Tola and Jair to the ladder and tell the children that they will need to memorize these three names along with all the others.

Approach to Lesson

Explain to the class that this is not a story about a God approved judge but it is a story about something that presumptuously tried to rule over Israel. It shows just how wicket some of the Israelites became when they stopped worshipping God. Let us learn about some of the very wicked things that took place.

Reinforcing Activities

1. This lesson can be taught with a flannelgraph. You will need a figure for Abimelech, the group of men at Shechem, the group of brothers who were slain, Jotham, and the group of people who were listening to him speak. You will need the olive tree, the fig tree, the grapevine, and the bramble bush, also. Great detail is not necessary and may only confuse the minds of the children. Have the class help you tell the story.

2. A good way to learn the names of the judges is with flashcards. The studetns should be able to recognize the names of each and can call out the name as you flash the card. Start out slowly and work up your speed gradually. Be sure all of the students are participating. This may call for a little individual attention for some of the shy children.

Applications

The main application that needs to be made is the fact that God will punish a person if he does wrong. Like Abimelech, his punishment may not come immediately, but God knows all and there is no way he can hide from Him. Even if he is not punished in this life, he will still have to answer to God on the day of judgment. This stresses the importance of repentance and asking God to forgive us of our wrong-doings.

Visual Displays

It would be a good idea, if you could have the fruit and the bramble to illustrate the story that Jotham told. You will need an olive, a fig, a grape, and a thorny bush of some sort. Let the children see and feel the difference in the fruit and the bramble. Help them to understand the meaning of this parable.

A bulletin board can show Jotham standing on a hill, telling his story, with pictures showing the different trees and the bramble. Let the children see how ugly the bramble is and that it can provide nothing like the other trees can.

Worksheets

Pass out worksheets and let the class complete them. They may exchange with a friend and write in the correct answers.

Extra! Extra! Shechem, Abimelech, king; men, killed, brothers; Jothan; crowned; Jotham, hill; story; olive, grapevine, bramble; small, thorns; Shechem, punished, wickedness.

The Story of Jepthah
Judg. 11

Lesson Aims

1. After studying this lesson, the student will see that even though Jephthah's vow cost him his daughter, he did not go back on it. We must not go back on any vows that we might make to the Lord, but we must also be careful what we do vow to God.

2. After studying this lesson and the previous lessons, the student should be able to give an example of a Bible character who acted out of faith in the Lord.

Preclass Activity

Dress the first student as Jephthah and tell each child a little about this judge. Perhaps you can take the children to the "cycle" bulletin board and go over this with them briefly.

Approach to Lesson

As you begin the lesson ask the students this question: "Have you ever told someone that you would do something for them and then, when the time came for you to do it, you did not want to and were sorry you had made that promise to them? Well, this is a story about a man who made a promise to God and ended up being sorry for making it. But this man did not go back on his promise to God. He did just what he had vowed. Let's look at this story and see what kind of a promise this man made to God."

Reinforcing Activities

1. Reinforcing this lesson may be a bit more difficult than others. Perhaps a filmstrip on the subject is available to you; if so, it would be effective. You can ask the students questions on the lesson and on previous lessons as a review. If they have any questions on the story you will need to answer them. Research Jephthah's vow in an Old Testament history book to help you better understand it and to help you answer any questions that the children may have concerning this portion of the story.

2. Have the student dressed as Jephthah hang his name rung on the ladder and tell the story to the class in his own words. If you happen to have any shy children "judges" be sure to help them at this point. Do not embarrass them, but encourage them so they will feel a bit more at ease.

Applications

The main point in this lesson is the vow which Jephthah made to God, and the results of it. The class should understand that Jephthah did not make this vow with the intention of making a human sacrifice. He did, however, keep his vow to God even though he had to kill his daughter. This shows not only the importance of keeping our promises, but also being careful to think carefully about the promises we do make, not only to other people, but to our Lord.

Visual Displays

A bulletin board can be constructed showing Jephthah's daughter running out to meet him on his return from battle. You may also have a bulletin board or perhaps some pictures contrasting the ways in which the people of the Old Testament worshipped God (sacrifices, religious feasts) and the ways in which we worship Him (Lord's supper, etc.).

Worksheets

Hand out the worksheets and let the children complete them. They will each need a Bible for the Bible Practice worksheet. If they do not have their own Bibles, you will need to provide them. If they have done a good job of memorizing their memory verses, they will not even need to use their Bibles. Perhaps they can exchange with a friend to check the answers.

Picture Words: 1. Jepthah; 2. Leader; 3. Daughter; 4. Judge.

Bible Practice: 1. Judg. 9:15; 2. Judg. 11:31; 3. Judg. 6:23; 4. Judg. 4:3; 5. Judg. 3:9; 6. Judg. 8:23; 7. Matt. 4:10.

The Judge Who Made Riddles
Judg. 13; 14:15-20

Lesson Aims

1. The student will see the importance of carefully choosing his friends. Even though we come in contact with worldly people in almost everything we do, we need to choose good people for our close associates. Careful choosing will help prevent us from being wrongly influenced by our peers.

2. After studying this lesson the student should begin to realize the full potential of Samson's strength as he killed the lion bare-handed. In the next lesson, we will learn the source of Samson's strength.

Preclass Activity

Dress the first student as Samson and pin on his name tag. Perhaps you can have a picture of Samson wrestling with the lion to show the class the strength of Samson.

Approach to Lesson

As you begin your lesson you may wish to start it off with a riddle or two of your own. Perhaps you can tell a riddle that would help them review the previous lesson. Make it an easy one like, "I'm thinking of a man who was so wicked that he killed all of his brothers except one." Or, "I'm thinking of a kind of bush that is ugly, thorny and not at all useful." After the class answers the riddles, tell them that this lesson is about a man who told a riddle that was rather hard to figure out. Let us take a look at this man and find out what that hard riddle was all about.

Reinforcing Activities

1. This lesson can be effectively taught with a flannelgraph. You will need figures for Samson, his parents, a lion, the Philistine Woman, and a group of Philistine men. Be sure to picture Samson with long hair. Use scenery and put a lot of enthusiasm into this story as it is an interesting and exciting story for these children. Let the class help you tell the story so they can become familiar with it in their own way.

2. Before your student who is dressed as Samson puts his name rung on the ladder, you will need to add the names of Ibzar, Elon, and Abdon to the ladder. These are three more judges who are mentioned in the Bible but regarding whom there is no further information. The class should commit these names to memory also. Have your student dressed as Samson hang his rung on the ladder as he tells the story briefly in his own words.

Applications

Samson was basically a good, godly man, but he did have some faults that got him into trouble. He was not very cautious in choosig his friends. We must be very careful with whom we choose to associate. Bad friends can influence us to do evil things (1 Cor. 15:33). Also, if we are seen associating with worldly people then others will think badly of us and our Christian influence on them will be damaged.

Visual Displays

A bulletin board can show Samson fighting with the lion on one side and coming across the lion with honey in it on the other side. Perhaps you can have some honey available to the children for them to see and taste. Explain to them that this was a rather unusual place for bees to produce honey since they normally build hives in trees. Continue with some more riddles pertaining to this and past lessons to help the children remember.

Worksheets

Hand out worksheets and allow time for children to do them. As they work on those, you can be checking their student books to see if they have completed their homework. Go over the answers in class if you wish.

Riddles: 1. angel; 2. Samson's parents; 3. lion; 4. bees; 5. riddle; 6. the girl Samson wanted to marry; 7. Samson.

True or False: 1. False; 2. True; 3. True; 4. False; 5. False; 6. True; 7. False; 8. True; 9. True; 10. False.

The Strongest Man
Judg. 15; 16
Lesson Aims

1. The student will again see the importance of choosing his friends carefully. Samson once again fell in love with a Philistine woman and truly paid for his mistake. He should have learned from the first time he did this, but apparently he did not. We may, at times, choose bad friends and have trouble because of that choice but we must learn from mistakes like this that we have to be more cautious.

2. The student will learn that even though Samson was a very strong man, he did not use his strength in good ways all of the time. He used his strength for revenge and on foolish things instead of using it to help his people. Returning evil for evil is never right.

Preclass Activity

You will not need to dress anyone as Samson since his name rung is already on the ladder. As the students come to class, you can show them some pictures to remind them of the last story about Samson and to prepare them for further information on the feats of Samson.

Approach to Lesson

The best way to approach this lesson is to have a short review of the last lesson. Ask the students some questions about the last story to see how much they remember and to refresh their memories. Today they will learn the reason Samson had great strength and how he had trouble with this great strength that he had.

Reinforcing Activities

1. A flannelgraph would be an effective way to teach this lesson, if it is taught with enthusiasm. A filmstrip would be very helpful if there is one available to you. The children will enjoy these episodes and will rejoice in the triumph of their hero over his enemies. They should remember that the Philistines were wicked people who should be punished. Yet, they must also recognize Samson's wrong doing.

2. Quiz the students with some questions about both of the stories on Samson. Be sure they have the events in the proper order and that they do not get them confused. Write some key words on the marker board and let them build a story around them.

Applications

When the Lord gives us special talents we need to use them to help others and to glorify His name. Using them foolishly and in wrong ways is not what God intended. As we have learned, Samson did not use his talents in the right way; he paid with his life for that mistake. We will pay for the same kinds of mistakes, if we are guilty of making them.

Visual Displays

A bulletin board can be made depicting Samson in any one of the scenes described in the lesson. You can show Samson with the foxes, with the jawbone of the donkey, breaking loose the ropes on his arms, carrying away the gates of the city, or pushing against the pillars of the house. This side of the board can show Samson when he was very strong; the other side of the board can show Samson when he was weak (such as Samson with his hair cut short, his eyes put out and working hard in the mill). Be sure that the students understand that Samson did not get his strength from his hair but that it came from God upon the condition that he not cut his hair.

Worksheets

Pass out the worksheets and allow time for completion. Perhaps you can use one of them as a quiz and collect it after they have finished. Return it to them at the next class.

Samson's Strength: ropes; jawbone; swarm; secret; lion; firebrands; bees; foxes; gate; riddle; Delilah; honey; angry; Philistine; hair.

Code Words: *Samson was a very strong man.*

A Woman Who Left Her Idols
Ruth 1

Lesson Aims

1. After studying this lesson, the student will see that he can do right and obey God even though most people around him may be very wicked.

2. The student will learn that although many of the Israelites were wicked much of the time, a few of them lived faithfully always, such as Naomi.

Preclass Activity

Since there is no judge in this particular lesson, you will not have a rung for the ladder. You may still wish to dress one of the girls as Ruth or Naomi and tell the students a little bit about these two women as they come to class. Tell them how they were related and how loyal Ruth was to her mother-in-law. Explain the meaning of loyality.

Approach to Lesson

This is a story about a woman who lived among people who worshipped idols. She never forgot God and continued to worship only Him. She was an older woman and had a young daughter-in-law whom she loved. This daughter-in-law worshipped idols. We shall learn in this story how this young woman came to worship the only true God.

Reinforcing Activities

1. This would be a good lesson to use pipe cleaner figures with. You will need a figure for the three women and some mules for them to ride on their journey across the land. Have one town set up as the town that they leave and one town set up as the town to which they are going. Tell the story as you move the figures across the sand (if available to you). Carry on a conversation between the women as they travel. Have a group of people in Bethlehem to welcome the women as they arrive in the city.

2. Draw a map on the marker board and trace the journey that Naomi and Ruth took. Show some of the neighboring countries that have been mentioned in previous lessons to give the children an idea of where these events took place.

Applications

When Ruth learned that she was doing wrong to worship idols, she was brave enough to turn her back to them and start worshipping the true and living God. We must also have enough courage to turn our backs on the sins of the world and do the things that God wants us to do. People may try to influence us to do wrong, but if we are strong in our beliefs, then we will be able to resist temptation and do the right things.

Visual Displays

The use of pipe cleaner figures is one of your visual displays as well as the map. Prepare a bulletin board showing Ruth turning from the idols to God or the two women entering into the city of Bethlehem and being welcomed by a group of people. Show pictures of older women and of younger women so the class will be able to tell the difference between Ruth and Naomi and have the proper image in their minds.

Worksheets

Hand out worksheets in class and let the children complete them. Perhaps you can copy the crossword puzzle on the marker board and let the class help you fill in the spaces.

Crossword: Across: 1. Moab; 2. Elimelech; 3. Ruth; 4. famine; 5. Naomi; 6. happiness. Down: 1. Bethlehem; 2. Orpah; 3. sons.

The scrambled verse is the memory verse.

Judge Review: 1. Othniel; 2. Deborah; 3. Ehud; 4. Samson; 5. Gideon; 6. Jephthah.

Ruth Finds a Home and Happiness
Ruth 2:1-13; 4:13-17

Lesson Aims

1. God blessed Ruth and Naomi and guided them because they were good women and obeyed God. God will bless us and guide our lives, if we will put our trust in Him and obey His will.

2. The student will see that Ruth was rewarded for her courage in leaving her old home and idols and coming to serve God. God gave her a good home and happiness; she became the great-grandmother of David. We will be rewarded if we will turn from evil and follow God. We will be happy and secure in the knowledge that God will take care of us.

Preclass Activity

As the children come in, show them a table where you have placed some wheat and some pictures that show people gathering wheat. They will delight in seeing and touching the grain and you can take a moment to tell them a little about gleaning.

Approach to Lesson

The best way to approach this lesson would be to review the previous lesson, recounting the journey that Ruth and Naomi took. Ask a few basic questions to refresh their memories and to see what they have retained. After Ruth came to her new home, many wonderful things happened to her. Let us learn about some of these nice happenings.

Reinforcing Activities

1. This would be a good lesson for role-playing. You will need someone to play Ruth, Naomi, and Boaz; the others can be workers in the fields. Let the children help tell the story as they act it out. Have some props such as the grain, something to put it in, and a table where Ruth and Boaz can sit to have lunch. If there is time, act it out a second time and let some of the actors change roles.

2. Have several pictures of the events of this story and the previous lesson. As you show them, have the children take turns explaining what is happening in the picture and also put them in correct chronological order.

Applications

The memory verse is truly the applications of this story. If we will only have trust in the Lord, then He will give us full reward. We may not receive this reward immediately or in large numbers while here on earth, but our reward in heaven will be great.

Visual Displays

Have a bulletin board showing Ruth gleaning in the field of Boaz and perhaps have Boaz watching her. On the other side of the board, show Ruth and Boaz together with the baby Obed in Ruth's arms. Again show the pictures of the people gathering grain and be sure the children understand what "gleaning" is.

Worksheets

Hand out worksheets and allow time for completion. Go over the answers together in class or collect the papers and check them at home; return them to the children at their next class period. Discuss the worksheets that they did at home in their books. As they tell you ways to show God you care for Him and ways He cares for you, list them on the marker board. Perhaps you can collect their pictures of Ruth and hang them in the room where they can be admired by all.

The Son Who Came in Answer to Prayer
1 Sam. 1:6-28; 2:18-21; 3

Lesson Aims

1. After studying this lesson the class will see that there are ways in which a child can serve God. Samuel served God by working in the tabernacle. We can serve God by obeying our parents, studying our Bible, telling others about Jesus, etc.

2. The student should, by now, be able to recite the five-step cycle of Israel's obedience to God and to give an example of each step in the cycle from the stories they have studied thus far.

Preclass Activity

You may dress the first student as Eli and pin his name tag on him. Tell the others a little about Eli but explain to them that not much history is known about Eli. When the Bible introduces Eli, he is already the judge of Israel and is living in the tabernacle as a priests.

Approach to Lesson

Even though the judge mentioned in this lesson is Eli, the story is basically about a little boy who came to live with Eli near the tabernacle and to serve the Lord. Let us look at this together and see what part Eli played in the life of this little boy.

Reinforcing Activities

1. This lesson can be taught effectively with role-playing. Have some one play the part of Hannah, Eli, Samuel, and, if necessary, Elkanah. Have an area of the room as the tabernacle and another area as the country where Hannah and Elkanah live. Have them travel to the tabernacle where Hannah prayed for a son. After Samuel is grown, have him move to the tabernacle. Each time thereafter have Hannah bring him a robe that she has made. Let the children tell the story in conversation as if they were truly speaking as the Bible characters.

2. Have the child dressed as Eli place his name rung on the ladder and briefly tell the story in his own words. Ask the students a few easy questions to test their retention.

Applications

As stated in the lesson aims, the student needs to realize the ways in which he can serve the Lord while he is yet a child. Perhaps you can ask the class ways in which they, as children, can be pleasing to God and make a list on the marker board. Emphasize to them that they must apply these actions to their everyday lives and must always seek to do what is right in the sight of God.

Visual Displays

Have a drawing or picture of the tabernacle where Samuel lived and explain to the children what Samuel did while he was in the tabernacle. He helped Eli take care of the building and did whatever Eli told him to do in order to serve the Lord.

Have a bulletin board showing Hannah praying to God for a son on one side and the body Samuel in the tabernacle on the other side. Hannah had her prayers answered because she was a woman who was a faithful servant to the Lord.

Worksheets

After the lesson, hand out the worksheets and let the children complete them. Have them exchange with a friend to check their answers. Make a list on the marker board of the ways in which the children feel that they served God this past week. Be sure to talk about any ways that were not listed and impress the importance of serving God in all that we do every day.

The Last Judge of Israel
1 Sam. 4:1-18; 7:1-15

Lesson Aims

1. The student will be able to recite from memory the names of the fifteen judges of Israel in the order of their appearance.

2. The student will be able to give two or three examples from the Old Testament where a person acted out of faith in the Lord.

Preclass Activity

Have the first student dress as Samuel and tell the students as they arrive that this is the last lesson and today they will hear the story about the last judge of Israel.

Approach to Lesson

Review the last lesson and ask the class some questions about it in order to get them reacquainted with Samuel and Eli. Today we will be doing a bit of reviewing over the past judges of Israel, but first we want to study the last judge of Israel and see how he became judge.

Reinforcing Activities

1. This lesson can be taught well with the use of a flannelgraph. You will need figures for Samuel, Eli, the Philistine army, the ark of God, the soldier who delivered the bad news to Eli, and, perhaps, the two sons of Eli. Put enthusiasm into this lesson and point out the cycle that the Israelites fell into again. It seems that the Israelites would never learn that they must obey God and worship only Him.

2. Have the student dressed as Samuel go to the ladder and hang his name rung upon it. At this time, go over all the judges with the children and ask them to name each one in order (without looking) as you write them on the marker board.

Applications

As we go about our daily activities and trials, we must always look to God for our guidance. We must always obey Him and worship Him alone. We must put our faith in Him and trust that He will care for us, if we will just do His will and always be an example to others. If we do wrong, then we must pray to Him for forgiveness and strive to do what is right.

Visual Displays

Have a picture from each previous lesson and ask very basic questions about each one. Clear up any questions that they may have at this time. Go over the cycle of history of the Israelites and ask for examples of each step. Try to get all the children involved in this so you can be sure each one knows the material he should. Do not let one or two children monopolize the questions.

Have a bulletin board depicting scenes from each previous lesson and have the class tell you which lesson they come from.

Worksheets

Hand out worksheets and allow time for completion. The students may exchange papers to check their answers. Be sure to check their books to see that they have done all of the work in them. One more time, go over the cycle of obedience.

Judges In Israel: J. Jephthah; U. Ehud; D. Gideon; G. Shamgar; E. Deborah; S. Samson; I. Eli; N. Abdon; I. Ibzan; S. Samuel; R. Jair; A. Tola; E. Othniel; L. Elon.

Bible Practice: Ruth 1:16; Judg. 14:14; 1 Sam. 1:28; 1 Sam. 7:3; Judg. 16:28, Ruth 2:12.